T0028717

I WILL GO WITH THEE
AND BE THY GUIDE,
IN THY MOST NEED
TO GO BY THY SIDE

EVERYMAN'S LIBRARY
POCKET POETS

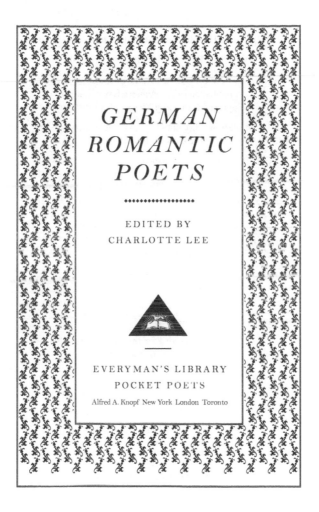

GERMAN ROMANTIC POETS

••••••••••••••••••

EDITED BY
CHARLOTTE LEE

EVERYMAN'S LIBRARY
POCKET POETS

Alfred A. Knopf New York London Toronto

THIS IS A BORZOI BOOK
PUBLISHED BY ALFRED A. KNOPF

This selection by Charlotte Lee
first published in Everyman's Library, 2024
Copyright © 2024 by Everyman's Library

everymanslibrary.com
www.everymanslibrary.co.uk

ISBN 978-1-101-90835-8 (US)
978-1-84159-831-4 (UK)

A CIP catalogue record for this book is available
from the British Library

Typography by Peter B. Willberg

Typeset in the UK by Input Data Services Ltd,
Bridgwater, Somerset

Printed and bound in Germany
by GGP Media GmbH, Pössneck

CONTENTS

Foreword 13

GOTTFRIED AUGUST BÜRGER (1747–94)
from William and Helen (Lenore) 23

JOHANN WOLFGANG GOETHE (1749–1832)
May Song (Mailied) 29
Welcome and Farewell
(Willkommen und Abschied) 31
Rosebud in the Heather (Heidenröslein) 33
Prometheus (Prometheus) 34
Ganymede (Ganymed) 37
My Peace is Gone (Meine Ruh ist hin)
from *Faust* 39
The Elf King (Erlkönig) 41
Wanderer's Night Song (Wandrers Nachtlied) 43
Another Night Song (Ein Gleiches) 43
Mignon (Kennst du das Land)
from *Wilhelm Meisters Lehrjahre* 44
Immense Astonishment
(Mächtiges Überraschen) 45
Ecstatic Longing (Selige Sehnsucht) 46

FRIEDRICH SCHILLER (1759–1805)
The Ideal and Life (Das Ideal und das Leben) 49
Evening (Der Abend) 52

The Visit of the Gods (Dithyrambe)   53
The Maiden's Plaint (Des Mädchens Klage)   55
Nenia (Nänie)   57
Mountain Song (Berglied)   58

AUGUST WILHELM SCHLEGEL (1767–1845)
   The Sonnet (Das Sonett)   63
   Evening Song for the Distant Beloved
     (Abendlied für die Entfernte)   64

FRIEDRICH HÖLDERLIN (1770–1843)
   In the Morning (Des Morgens)   69
   from Bread and Wine (Brod und Wein)   70
   Ganymede (Ganymed)   72
   The Half of Life (Hälfte des Lebens)   74
   Remembrance (Andenken)   75
   The Ister (Der Ister)   78

SOPHIE MEREAU (1770–1806)
   Spring (Frühling)   83
   To a Trellised Tree
     (An einen Baum am Spalier)   86

FRIEDRICH VON HARDENBERG ('NOVALIS', 1772–1801)
   Sacred Songs (Geistliche Lieder)
     X. There Come Such Troubled Hours
       (Es gibt so bange Zeiten)   89

XV. Maria
(Ich sehe dich in tausend Bildern) 91
Hymns to Night (Hymnen an die Nacht)
II. 92
VI. Longing for Death
(Sehnsucht nach dem Tode).. 93
The Hermit's Song (Gern verweil ich noch
im Tale) from *Heinrich von Ofterdingen* .. 96

FRIEDRICH SCHLEGEL (1772–1829)
The Boatman (Der Schiffer) 99
Sunset (Abendröte) 100

LUDWIG TIECK (1773–1853)
Sweet Darling, Rest in the Shade
(Schlaflied) 103
Wonder of Love (Wunder der Liebe) 104
Love (Liebe) 106

CLEMENS BRENTANO (1778–1842)
Slumber Song (Wiegenlied) 109
Evening Serenade (Abendständchen) 110
Lore Lay (Lore Lay) 111
The Spinstress' Song (Der Spinnerin Lied) .. 116
The Forest (O kühler Wald) 118
Lord! Within Thy Peace I Rest Me
(Herr! Ich steh in deinem Frieden) 119

Holy Night, Holy Night! (Heil'ge Nacht,
    heil'ge Nacht!)   120
Echoes of Beethoven's Music
    (Nachklänge Beethovenscher Musik)   121

KAROLINE VON GÜNDERRODE (1780–1806)
  The Kiss in the Dream
    (Der Kuss im Traume)..   127
  Dedication (Zueignung)   128
  The Prime Lament (Die eine Klage)   129
  Bright Red (Hochroth)   131
  The Balloonist (Der Luftschiffer)   132

ADALBERT VON CHAMISSO (1781–1838)
  The Soldier (Der Soldat)   135
  Lord Byron's Last Love
    (Lord Byrons letzte Liebe)   136

JUSTINUS KERNER (1786–1862)
  Oppressive Dream
    (Der schwere Traum [Ikaros])   141
  The Saw-Mill
    (Der Wandrer in der Sägemühle)   142

LUDWIG UHLAND (1787–1862)
  The Chapel (Die Kapelle)..   147
  The Dream (Der Traum)..   148
  The Smith (Der Schmied)   149

Spring Faith (Frühlingsglaube) 150
The Gossamer (Der Sommerfaden) 151
On the Death of a Child
    (Auf den Tod eines Kindes) 152

JOSEPH FREIHERR VON EICHENDORFF (1788–1857)
    The Broken Ring (Das zerbrochene Ringlein) 155
    Dialogue in the Forest (Waldgespräch) 156
    The Joyful Traveller
        (Der frohe Wandersmann) 157
    Prague Students' Song
        (Wanderlied der Prager Studenten) 158
    Evening (Abend) 100
    Nocturne (Nachts) 161
    On the Death of My Child
        (Auf meines Kindes Tod) 162
    Night (Die Nachtblume) 163
    Longing (Sehnsucht) 164
    Night of Moon (Mondnacht) 165
    The Hermit (Der Einsiedler) 166
    Wishing Wand (Wünschelrute) 167
    Death Wish (Todeslust) 168
    Memento mori (Memento mori!) 169
    The Poet Walks Abroad
        (Wandernder Dichter) 170
    Old Age (Das Alter) 171

FRIEDRICH RÜCKERT (1788–1866)

    My Soul, My Heart (Du meine Seele) 175

    O Stop with Me (Du bist die Ruh) 176

    'Now the sun prepares to rise as brightly'

        ('Nun will die Sonn' so hell aufgeh'n'). . . . 177

    Closing Song (Schlusslied) 178

WILHELM MÜLLER (1794–1827)

    The Journeyman's Song (Wanderschaft) . . 181

    The Linden Tree (Der Lindenbaum) 183

AUGUST GRAF VON PLATEN-HALLERMÜNDE

    (1797–1848)

    Truest of Sages are You to Me

        (Du bist der wahre Weise mir) 187

    Fain Would I Live in Safest Freedom

        (Ich möchte gern mich frei bewahren). . . . 188

    Venetian Sonnets (Sonette aus Venedig)

        II. 189

        VIII. 190

ANNETTE VON DROSTE-HÜLSHOFF (1797–1848)

    The Pond (Der Weiher) 193

    The House in the Heath

        (Das Haus in der Heide) 194

    In the Grass (Im Grase) 196

    Moonrise (Mondesaufgang) 198

HEINRICH HEINE (1797–1856)

'In May, the magic month of May'
('Im wunderschönen Monat Mai').. 203
'On wings of song' ('Flügeln des Gesanges') 204
'The lotus flower' ('Die Lotosblume ängstigt') 205
'A Youth Once Loved'
('Ein Jüngling liebt ein Mädchen') 206
'They talked of love and devotion'
('Sie saßen und tranken am Teetisch') .. 207
Lorelei ('Ich weiß nicht, was soll es bedeuten') 208
'The night is still, the streets are dumb'
('Still ist die Nacht, es ruhen die Gassen').. 210
'I called the devil and he came'
('Ich rief den Teufel, und er kam') 211
'Ah, those eyes'
('Ach die Augen sind es wieder') 212
Sea Apparition (Seegespenst) 213
Memorial Day (Gedächtnisfeier).. 216
The Silesian Weavers
(Die schlesischen Weber) 217
Babylonian Sorrows (Babylonische Sorgen) .. 219

NIKOLAUS LENAU (1802–50)

The Oak Grove (Der Eichwald) 223
'The evening wind in the treetops'
('Der Nachtwind hat in den Bäumen').. .. 224
Plea (Bitte) 225

EDUARD MÖRIKE (1804–75)

   In Spring (Im Frühling)   229
   To an Aeolian Harp (An eine Äolsharfe)   231
   The Beautiful Beech Tree (Die schöne Buche)   233
   On a Lamp (Auf eine Lampe)   235
   Reflect, My Soul (Denk' es, o Seele)   236
   At Midnight (Um Mitternacht)   237
   To a Christmas-Rose (Auf eine Christblume)   238
   Prayer (Gebet)   240

RICHARD WAGNER (1813–88)

   So let us die (So stürben wir)
      from *Tristan and Isolde*   243

Acknowledgments and Sources   246

FOREWORD

The convention in scholarship is to see German Romanticism as starting in the 1790s, with the Schlegel brothers and their circle in Jena, and ending in the 1820s, part way through the career of the great poet Heinrich Heine. This anthology begins earlier and finishes later, thereby incorporating crucial influences – without which Romanticism cannot be properly understood – and giving an idea of the legacy of the movement. This is particularly helpful if we wish to develop a sense of the place of German poetry in the broader context of European Romanticism. Indeed, it is perhaps more accurate, though less elegant, to speak of *Romanticisms*. These flowered at different times. French literary Romanticism, for example, reached its high point a little later than German literary Romanticism. Romantic movements in the various artistic media also had their own trajectories: in Germany, the Romantic era in music peaked later than in literature, and extended as late as Wagner, Bruckner and Mahler. A more generous understanding of the boundaries of German literary Romanticism, therefore, also helps us to understand how developments in poetry relate to those in other art forms.

This collection opens with an excerpt from *William and Helen*, Sir Walter Scott's translation of *Lenore*, a ballad by Gottfried August Bürger. *Lenore* was very influential in Britain and elsewhere, and it was also in some ways the source of the trend for ballads which the Romantics adopted, via Goethe. The Early Romantic circle from Jena is represented in the poetry of August Wilhelm and Friedrich Schlegel, Novalis, Ludwig Tieck and Sophie Mereau. The Schlegel brothers provided much of the theoretical impetus behind Early Romanticism, and August Wilhelm's erudite contributions were particularly important for developments in the lyric. Also of that generation, and kindred to an extent in philosophical terms, was Friedrich Hölderlin, one of the most complex but most brilliant writers in the German language. Next come Clemens Brentano and Karoline von Günderrode. Günderrode was a rare philosophical and poetic talent, whose work is rooted in its time, yet also highly distinctive. Brentano was an especially gifted lyric poet, who was prolific on his own terms, and who also collaborated with Achim von Arnim to produce the famous folk collection *Des Knaben Wunderhorn* (extracts of which were later set to music by Gustav Mahler). The predilection for folk-style poetry – which was often highly artful – goes back several decades to the influence of Johann Gottfried Herder, and before him, Thomas Percy in England. Goethe's 'Heidenröslein' is a particularly famous example of this approach.

Joseph Freiherr von Eichendorff represents the peak of later Romantic poetry. He had become closely acquainted with Arnim and Brentano in Heidelberg, and ultimately took Romanticism in a very different direction from that envisioned by the Schlegel brothers. Several other poets of roughly Eichendorff's generation, such as Adalbert von Chamisso, Justinus Kerner and Ludwig Uhland are also included: they were all popular in Germany and, very often, were beloved of Victorian translators too. Together with Eichendorff, Heinrich Heine is often considered the Romantic poet *par excellence*. From early in his career, however, his work is poised between admiration for and scepticism of the movement, and his critical distance becomes more marked later on. Although this selection is tipped towards the earlier part of his œuvre, the later, in some ways anti-Romantic part is also represented. With Heine, we have reached the notional end of the Romantic period proper, and Eichendorff was plagued in his later years by the sense that he was becoming outmoded; yet plenty of writers, such as the Austrian poet Nikolaus Lenau, continued to compose in the Romantic idiom. Annette von Droste-Hülshoff and Eduard Mörike are sometimes described as post-Romantic poets, meaning that their poetry still bears the stamp of the Romantic era but, with their own innovations, they also ushered in a new era, even anticipating Modernism. With Richard Wagner, finally, the Romantic legacy gathered new momentum: Wagner, who wrote his own libretti, channeled the influence of literary Romanticism into his *Gesamtkunstwerk* (total art work), which moves Romantic opera into modern music.

Germany's most famous writer and polymath, Johann Wolfgang Goethe, occupies a singular place in all this. There has been a tendency to see Goethe as distinct from the Romantics; for some, his approach was even antithetical to Romanticism. Something similar obtains for his great friend and collaborator, Friedrich Schiller. There are evident differences between their work and (say) that of the Schlegels. Yet there was significant mutual influence, in particular between Goethe and the first generation of Romantics, and both Goethe and Schiller shared many of the intellectual interests which drove Early Romanticism. Indeed, with his early pre-Romantic works such as 'May Song' (1771) and *The Sorrows of Young Werther* (1774), Goethe was a major catalyst for what was to come. Moreover, the second part of his *Faust*, which was written in old age and published posthumously in 1832, continues and further radicalizes 'Romantic' trends even after other major figures in the movement had died or moved on. In addition, of course, Goethe's influence on Romantic *music* was crucial: his poetry makes up a significant part of the corpus of Lieder (songs) by Schubert, Schumann and others. Readers may also recognize works in this collection by other poets – the Schlegel brothers, Uhland, Eichendorff, Friedrich Rückert, Heine and Wilhelm Müller – which have likewise been immortalized in music. Schiller, for his part, is perhaps best known for his works for the stage (many of which are also in verse, in iambic pentameter); but his poetry is just as striking for its combination of sculpted elegance and psychological intensity.

Various motifs and characters recur in this collection. The themes most commonly associated with Romantic poetry are love, death, night and nature – in particular the forests which to this day cover large areas of Germany. All these, accordingly, are prominent in this selection. In Eichendorff's 'Night of Moon', nature mysticism fuses with Christian faith, and the themes of love and death merge memorably in the excerpts from the end of Act Two of Wagner's *Tristan and Isolde*. Child mortality is a particularly poignant motif in the poetry of this period, and again, this is reflected here in poems by Goethe ('Erlkönig'), Uhland ('On the Death of a Child'), Eichendorff ('On the Death of My Child'), Rückert ('Now the sun prepares to rise as brightly') and Mörike ('To an Aeolian Harp'). Certain characters are also passed from poet to poet. The most famous is Lorelei, a female enchantress associated with the 132 metre-high rock of the same name on the right bank of the Rhine. An original invention of Brentano's ('Lore Lay'), she surfaces in many Romantic poems (see 'Dialogue in the Forest' by Eichendorff and 'Lorelei' by Heine in this collection), and became legend – indeed, her status in popular culture is such that it can come as a surprise to learn that she is a product of Romanticism rather than of more ancient folklore. This is an example of how convincing Romantic poets could be in their adoption of the 'folk' mode.

The formal range of German Romantic poetry is significant. The most common, as will be clear from this collection, is the four-line stanza. This broad category includes (but is not confined to) the ballad, a narrative form. Examples in this collection include Goethe's 'Erlkönig' and the various Lorelei poems. Some poets also wrote in freer or more idiosyncratic forms at points. In Novalis's *Hymns to Night*, we even have examples of prose poetry: this cycle of six begins with rhythmed prose and lifts gradually into full verse. In addition, the Romantic period was a time of experimentation with historical forms, such as the elegiac couplet or distich, derived from Greek and Latin poetry and consisting of a hexameter line followed by a pentameter line. This was given particular impetus in the 1790s by Goethe and Schiller (see, for example, 'Nenia') and taken up by others, above all by Hölderlin, who became the supreme exponent of the elegy (see 'Bread and Wine'). The boundaries between 'Romanticism' and 'Classicism' in German literature of this period are by no means as rigid as has often been claimed: the Schlegel brothers, for example, were enthusiastic about the revival of the classical elegy. An even bigger trend, however, was for the sonnet, spearheaded in the early 1800s by August Wilhelm Schlegel; a number of sonnets, accordingly, are given here. Finally, the collection includes two examples of the Persian-style ghazal: 'Closing Song' (Rückert) and 'Truest of Sages are You to Me' (August von Platen). The ghazal form consists of couplets, all of which end with the same rhyme-sound (AA, BA, CA, etc.). While Goethe's *West-östlicher Divan* (*West-Eastern Divan*) remains the best-known tribute to Persian poetry in German, other poets in fact went even deeper in their engagement with the language and its literary traditions. Both Rückert and Platen could read Persian fluently – Rückert, indeed, was Professor of Oriental Languages, as the discipline was then called – and both demonstrated considerable poetic skill in the many original ghazals that they composed.

The intricate rhymes and metres of the ghazal bring us to the difficulty of preserving form in translation. If the translator's attention to form is too blinkered, the 'argument' of the poem will suffer. So might its sound, in fact: hackneyed rhymes and forced metres are probably worse than a verse translation which feels prosy. On the other hand, if a translation retains little or nothing of the poem's original 'shape', the reader will have but a fraction of an impression of the source text. There is, of course, more to poetry than rhyme; but given that rhyme was an important resource for many

Romantic poets, preference has been given in this collection to translations which preserve this feature. Relaxing the demands of form in favour of a subtle representation of content can also lead to impressive renderings, however, and this approach to translating poetry is represented here too. The collection has been determined partly by the translations that exist, and there is more available for some poets than for others; but the hope is that the work of the many great translators and scholars of German represented here will convey a vivid sense of what Romanticism was and is.

Some poems are taken from larger collections (notably Heine's *Book of Songs*), but I have only included the titles of short cycles here (such as Novalis's *Hymns to Night*), because these are more crucial to the understanding of a given poem. Titles have been given in both English and German to make it easier for readers to trace the original should they so wish.

I am grateful to Nicholas Boyle, John Guthrie, Peter Hutchinson and Joanna Raisbeck for their ideas for this selection, and to Roger Paulin for providing new translations of poems by August Wilhelm Schlegel, Ludwig Tieck and Eduard Mörike.

CHARLOTTE LEE

GOTTFRIED AUGUST BÜRGER

(1747–94)

from WILLIAM AND HELEN
(LENORE)

XXXIII
'To-night – to-night a hundred miles! –
O dearest William, stay!
The bell strikes twelve – dark, dismal hour!
O wait, my love, till day!' –

XXXIV
'Look here, look here – the moon shines clear –
Full fast I ween we ride;
Mount and away! for ere the day
We reach our bridal bed.

XXXV
'The black barb snorts, the bridle rings;
Haste, busk, and boune, and seat thee!
The feast is made, the chamber spread,
The bridal guests await thee.' –

XXXVI
Strong love prevail'd: She busks, she bounes,
She mounts barb behind,
And round her darling William's waist
Her lily arms she twined.

XXXVII
And, hurry! hurry! off they rode,
As fast as fast might be;
Spurn'd from the courser's thundering heels
The flashing pebbles flee.

XXXVIII
And on the right, and on the left,
Ere they could snatch a view,
Fast, fast each mountain, mead, and plain,
And cot, and castle, flew.

XXXIX
'Sit fast – dost fear? – The moon shines clear –
Fleet goes my barb – keep hold!
Fear'st thou?' – 'O no!' she faintly said;
'But why so stern and cold?

XL
'What yonder rings? what yonder sings?
Why shrieks the owlet grey?' –
''Tis death-bells' clang, 'tis funeral song,
The body to the clay.

XLI

'With song and clang, at morrow's dawn,
Ye may inter the dead:
To-night I ride with my young bride,
To deck our bridal bed.

XLII

'Come with thy choir, thou coffin'd guest,
To swell our nuptial song!
Come, priest, to bless our marriage feast!
Come all, come all along!' –

XLIII

Ceased clang and song; down sunk the bier;
The shrouded corpse arose:
And, hurry! hurry! all the train
The thundering steed pursues.

XLIV

And, forward! forward! on they go;
High snorts the straining steed;
Thick pants the rider's labouring breath,
As headlong on they speed.

XLV

'O William, why this savage haste?
And where thy bridal bed?' –
''Tis distant far, low, damp, and chill,
And narrow, trustless maid.' –

XLVI

'No room for me?' – 'Enough for both; –
Speed, speed, my barb, thy course!'
O'er thundering bridge, through boiling surge
He drove the furious horse.

XLVII

Tramp! tramp! along the land they rode,
Splash! splash! along the sea;
The scourge is wight, the spur is bright,
The flashing pebbles flee.

JOHANN WOLFGANG GOETHE

(1749–1832)

MAY SONG
(MAILIED)
March 1771

How splendid nature
Shines all for me!
The sun, it sparkles!
Fields laugh with glee!

From all the branches
The blossoms push,
A thousand voices
From every bush

And joy and rapture
From every breast.
O earth, o sunshine,
O bliss, o zest,

O love, o love,
So golden bright
As clouds of morning
Upon that height,

On fresh fields richly
Your blessings spill,
With haze of blossom
The world you fill!

O girl my darling
How I love you!
Your eyes, how shining!
How you love too!

So loves the skylark
Its song on high
And morning flowers
The fragrant sky

As I am burning
With love for you
Who give me courage
And youth anew,

Give joy, set singing
And dancing free;
Be ever happy
As you love me.

WELCOME AND FAREWELL
(WILLKOMMEN UND ABSCHIED)

My heart beat fast, a horse! away!
Quicker than thought I am astride,
Earth now lulled by end of day,
Night hovering on the mountainside.
A robe of mist around him flung,
The oak a towering giant stood,
A hundred eyes of jet had sprung
From darkness in the bushy wood.

Atop a hill of cloud the moon
Shed piteous glimmers through the mist,
Softly the wind took flight, and soon
With horrible wings around me hissed.
Night made a thousand ghouls respire,
Of what I felt, a thousandth part —
My mind, what a consuming fire!
What a glow was in my heart!

You I saw, your look replied,
Your sweet felicity, my own,
My heart was with you, at your side,
I breathed for you, for you alone.
A blush was there, as if your face
A rosy hue of Spring had caught,

For me – ye gods! – this tenderness!
I hoped, and I deserved it not.

Yet soon the morning sun was there,
My heart, ah, shrank as leave I took:
How rapturous your kisses were,
What anguish then was in your look!
I left, you stood with downcast eyes,
In tears you saw me riding off:
Yet, to be loved, what happiness!
What happiness, ye gods, to love!

ROSEBUD IN THE HEATHER
(HEIDENRÖSLEIN)

Urchin saw a rose – a dear
Rosebud in the heather.
Fresh as dawn and morning-clear;
Ran up quick and stooped to peer,
Took his fill of pleasure.
Rosebud, rosebud, rosebud red,
Rosebud in the heather.

Urchin blurts: 'I'll pick you, though,
Rosebud in the heather!'
Rosebud: 'Then I'll stick you so
That there's no forgetting, no!
I'll not stand it, ever!'
Rosebud, rosebud, rosebud red,
Rosebud in the heather.

But the wild young fellow's torn
Rosebud from the heather.
Rose, she pricks him with her thorn;
Should she plead, or cry forlorn?
Makes no difference whether.
Rosebud, rosebud, rosebud red,
Rosebud in the heather.

Tr. John Frederick Nims

PROMETHEUS
(PROMETHEUS)

Cover your heaven, Zeus,
With cloudy vapors
And like a boy
Beheading thistles
Practice on oaks and mountain peaks –
Still you must leave
My earth intact
And my small hovel, which you did not build,
And this my hearth
Whose glowing heat
You envy me.

I know of nothing more wretched
Under the sun than you gods!
Meagerly you nourish
Your majesty
On dues of sacrifice
And breath of prayer
And would suffer want
But for children and beggars,
Poor hopeful fools.

Once too, a child,
Not knowing where to turn,
I raised bewildered eyes

Up to the sun, as if above there were
An ear to hear my complaint,
A heart like mine
To take pity on the oppressed.

Who helped me
Against the Titans' arrogance?
Who rescued me from death,
From slavery?
Did not my holy and glowing heart,
Unaided, accomplish all?
And did it not, young and good,
Cheated, glow thankfulness
For its safety to him, to the sleeper above?

I pay homage to you? For what?
Have you ever relieved
The burdened man's anguish?
Have you ever assuaged
The frightened man's tears?
Was it not omnipotent Time
That forged me into manhood,
And eternal Fate,
My masters and yours?

Or did you think perhaps
That I should hate this life,
Flee into deserts

Because not all
The blossoms of dream grew ripe?

Here I sit, forming men
In my image,
A race to resemble me:
To suffer, to weep,
To enjoy, to be glad –
And never to heed you,
Like me!

GANYMEDE
(GANYMED)

How in the brightness of morning,
All round me, you glow upon me,
Oh spring, oh my lover!
With the rapture of a thousand loves
It thrusts at my heart,
This sacred sense
Of your eternal ardour,
Oh infinite beauty!

Oh let me hold you
Here in my arms!

Ah, at your breast
I lie, I languish,
And your flowers, your grass,
They thrust at my heart.
You cool the burning
Thirst within me,
Sweet morning wind!
The nightingale calls to me,
Calls out in love from the misty valley.

I come, I come!
Oh where am I going?

Upwards, drawn upwards.
The clouds float down,
The clouds descend
To my love and my longing.
To me! To me!
Upwards, carried in their womb,
Embraced and embracing!
Borne aloft to your heart,
Oh father, lover of all!

.

MY PEACE IS GONE
(MEINE RUH IST HIN)
from *Faust*

GRETCHEN *at the spinning wheel, alone*

My peace is gone,
My heart is sore,
It's gone for ever
And evermore.

Whenever he
Is far away,
The world for me
Is cold and grey.

And my poor head
Is quite bemused,
My scattered wits
Are all confused.

My peace is gone,
My heart is sore,
It's gone for ever
And evermore.

It's him I look for
On the street,

It's only him
I go to meet.

And in his walk,
Such dignity.
His gracious talk
Bewitches me.

And when he smiles
At me, what bliss,
To feel his hand –
And ah, his kiss!

My peace is gone,
My heart is sore,
It's gone for ever
And evermore.

Here in my heart
I long for him,
And if I could
Belong to him,

I'd hold him and kiss him
All the day,
Though in his kisses
I'd melt away!

THE ELF KING
(ERLKÖNIG)

Who is riding so late on a night so wild?
A father is riding and carrying his child.
He holds the boy tight as he rides through the storm,
He grips him safely, he keeps him warm.

What's wrong, boy, why do you hide your face? –
Oh father, the Elf King's in that dark place!
Oh don't you see him, his robe and his crown? –
My son, it's the mists as the night comes down. –

'My dear child, come, come away with me!
Our games together, what games they'll be!
On the shore there are flowers, fine colours untold;
My mother will clothe you in cloth of gold.'

Oh father, oh father, oh can you not hear
What the Elf King is whispering into my ear? –
Hush, hush now, my son, all's well now, what's wrong?
It's the wind in the dry leaves singing its song. –

'Sweet boy, will you come, will you come my way?
My daughters shall wait on you night and day,
When it's dark, my daughters will dance in a ring,
You'll sleep when they rock you, you'll sleep when
        they sing.'

Oh father, oh father, oh do you not see
The Elf King's daughters looking at me? –
I see them, my son, I see all that's there:
It's the old willow-trees and their long grey hair. –

'I love you, your beauty has wakened my lust;
Little boy, I'll take you by force if I must.'
Oh father, oh father, don't let me go!
The Elf King has caught me, he hurts me so! –

The father shudders, he rides on fast,
With the poor moaning child he gets home at last,
He reaches his home with trouble and dread,
With the boy in his arms; but the boy is dead.

WANDERER'S NIGHT SONG
(WANDRERS NACHTLIED)

Thou that from the heavens art,
    Every pain and sorrow stillest,
And the doubly wretched heart
    Doubly with refreshment fillest,
I am weary with contending!
    Why this rapture and unrest?
Peace descending
    Come, ah, come into my breast!

ANOTHER NIGHT SONG
(EIN GLEICHES)

O'er all the hill-tops
    Is quiet now,
In all the tree-tops
    Hearest thou
Hardly a breath;
    The birds are asleep in the trees:
    Wait, soon like these
        Thou, too, shalt rest.

MIGNON
(KENNST DU DAS LAND)
from *Wilhelm Meisters Lehrjahre*

You know that land, her lemon groves in bloom?
Dark foliage of the orange, gold in gloom?
So soft a blowing air, so blue a sky
Over the myrtle hushed, the laurel high?
You know that land perhaps?
                              Oh that's the way
I'd go with you, my dearest – off today!

You know that house, how tall the pillars stand?
The halls all glossy, and the chambers grand?
The marble shapes that eye me, where I go:
'What's the world done, poor child, to hurt you so?'
You know the house perhaps?
                              Oh that's the way
I'd go with you, my guardian – off today!

You know that mountain and its cloudy track?
The drifting haze, the mule-clop echoing back?
– Old dragons and their brood in grottoes sprawl;
Each rock's a cliff; each brook, a waterfall.
You know the place perhaps?
                              Oh that's the way
Our journey goes! Good father, off today!

IMMENSE ASTONISHMENT
(MÄCHTIGES ÜBERRASCHEN)

A river from a cloud-wrapped chamber gone,
Of rock, and roaring to be one with ocean,
Much it reflects from deep to deep, its motion
Never relenting valleyward and on.

But with abrupt demoniacal force,
By forest, mountain, whirling wind pursued,
Oreas tumbles down into quietude,
And there she brims the bowl, impedes the course.

The wave breaks into spray, astonished, back
Uphill it washes, drinking itself always;
Its urge to join the Father hindered, too,

It rolls and rests, is dammed into a lake;
The constellations, mirrored, fix their gaze:
The flash of wave on rock, a life made new.

ECSTATIC LONGING
(SELIGE SEHNSUCHT)

Tell it to the wisest only,
For the mob will mock such learning:
I will praise the living creature
That can long for death by burning.

As the candle's quiet gleaming
Cools your nights of hot surrender,
You are touched by strange emotion,
Born again as you engender.

You have passed beyond the shadows:
Snatched aloft, you shall discover
New desire and higher union:
Thrall of darkness now is over.

Distance tires you not nor hinders,
On you come with fated flight
Till, poor moth, at last you perish
In the flame, in love with light.

Die into becoming! Grasp
This, or sad and weary
Shall your sojourn ever be
On the dark earth dreary.

FRIEDRICH SCHILLER

(1759–1805)

THE IDEAL AND LIFE

(DAS IDEAL UND DAS LEBEN)

Tranquil and pure as glass, forever clear,
Soft as a zephyr, unassailed by fear,
For the Olympian gods life gently flows.
The generations pass, moons wax and wane,
Immutable amid eternal bane,
For them, the gods, forever blooms the rose.
In human life a fearful course is run
Between the senses and peace of the soul.
But on the lofty brow of Saturn's son
These two unite to make one radiant whole.

If you would be like gods upon the earth
And wander freely in the realms of Death,
Pluck no morsels of his garden's fruit.
Safe to delight the eye in outward showing,
But perilous to taste what there is growing,
For having punishes desire's pursuit.
Even the Styx, entwined ninefold around her,
Cannot prevent Proserpine's return.
Once she has grasped the apple, it has bound her
To Hades for an everlasting sojourn.

The flesh alone is prey to those dark powers
Ever weaving at our destinies;
Freed of bondage to the hours,
Playmate of blissful entities,
The pure form rises to Elysian bowers,
Itself divine among divinities.
If you would soar as high upon its wings,
Cast off the terrors of mortality,
Flee from the narrowness of daily things
Into the realm of ideality.

There, young and free from any earthly stain,
Soaring in perfect being's high domain,
There is man's image of divinity,
As life's silent phantoms like bright gleams
Drift along beside the Stygian streams,
As, amid the field of heaven, she,
The Immortal, stood before descending
Into the mournful burial vaults below.
When in life the struggle seems unending,
Suddenly we sense sweet victory's glow.

When the spirit kindles with desire
To shape dead matter, lend it life's own fire,
To take crude mass and pass it on refined –
It must be done by straining every nerve;
Only unflinching constancy will serve
To subjugate the elements to Mind.
For Truth in her mysterious deep spring
Yields only to the one who spares no pain.
As marble only can be made to sing
Under the chisel's merciless refrain.

But once the shape of beauty has been found
All weight lies with the chips upon the ground.
And from the massive block, now free to rise,
Slender and light, as it were made of air,
Showing no trace of all the pangs and care,
The statue stands before enraptured eyes.
For all the doubts and struggles now have vanished
In the sureness of a victory,
And every single sign has now been banished
That spoke to us of human poverty.

EVENING
(DER ABEND)

Sink, irradiant god, the fields are thirsting
for the comforting dew, and men are fainting,
weakly struggle your horses –
let your bright chariot descend.

See her, who from the ocean's waves of crystal
smilingly beckons to you. Your heart discerns her.
Swiftly hasten the horses;
Tethys, the goddess, is she.

Quickly down from the chariot springs the driver
(Cupid seizes the reins) and soon he holds her,
Quietly the tired horses
drink from the fresh, cooling flood.

Up the evening sky with silent footsteps
mounts the sweet-scented night; behind her follows
Love. O rest now and love now!
Phoebus, the lover, shall rest.

THE VISIT OF THE GODS
(DITHYRAMBE)

(*Imitated from Schiller*)

    Never, believe me,
    Appear the Immortals,
      Never alone:
Scarce had I welcomed the sorrow-beguiler,
Iacchus! but in came boy Cupid the smiler;
Lo! Phoebus the glorious descends from his throne!
They advance, they float in, the Olympians all!
    With divinities fills my
      Terrestrial hall!

    How shall I yield you
    Due entertainment,
      Celestial quire?
Me rather, bright guests! with your wings of
    upbuoyance,
Bear aloft to your homes, to your banquets of joyance,
That the roofs of Olympus may echo my lyre!
Hah! we mount! on their pinions they waft up my soul!
    O give me the nectar!
      O fill me the bowl!

Give him the nectar!
Pour out for the poet,
Hebe! pour free!
Quicken his eyes with celestial dew,
That Styx the detested no more he may view,
And like one of us Gods may conceit him to be!
Thanks, Hebe! I quaff it! Io Paean, I cry!
The wine of the Immortals
Forbids me to die!

THE MAIDEN'S PLAINT
(DES MÄDCHENS KLAGE)

The forestpines groan –
The dim clouds are flitting –
The Maiden is sitting
On the green shore alone,
The surges are broken with might, with might,
And her sighs are pour'd on the desert Night,
And tears are troubling her eye.

'All, all is o'er:
The heart is destroyed –
The world is a void –
It can yield me no more.
Then, Master of Life, take back thy boon:
I have tasted such bliss as is under the moon:
I have lived – I have loved – I would die!'

Thy tears, O Forsaken!
Are gushing in vain;
Thy wail shall not waken
The Buried again:
But all that is left for the desolate bosom,
The flower of whose Love has been blasted in
       blossom,
Be granted to thee from on high!

Then pour like a river
Thy tears without number!
The Buried can never
Be wept from their slumber:
But the luxury dear to the Broken-hearted,
When the sweet enchantment of Love hath departed,
Be thine – the tear and the sigh!

NENIA

(NÄNIE)

Also the beautiful dies. — Its spell binds all men
and immortals
Save one: the Stygian Zeus. Armored in steel is
his breast.
Once, only did soften a lover the ruler of Hades.
Yet, ere the threshold was reached, sternly he
canceled his gift.
As Aphrodite stills not the gaping wounds of Adonis
Which on the beautiful youth, hunted, the wild
boar inflicts,
So the immortal Thetis saves not her divine son
Achilles
When at the Scaean Gate, falling, he meets with
his fate.
But from the sea she arises with all the daughters of
Nereus,
And they intone their lament for her transfigured
son.
Lo, all the gods now are weeping and weeping is
every goddess
That the beautiful wanes, that the perfect must die.
Glory is also to be a song of sorrow of loved ones,
For, what is vulgar goes down songless to echoless
depths.

MOUNTAIN SONG
(BERGLIED)

The pathway clings to the precipice wall
and passes from danger to danger;
It's guarded by giants, enormously tall,
which threaten the wandering stranger.
And who would not waken the lion that dwells
on the height will walk softly this highway of hells.

The fearful depth of the chasm is spanned
by an arch that hangs in the sky,
a bridge not constructed by human hand;
no man would have ventured so high.
The torrent roars underneath early and late,
but the bridge is untouched by its violent hate.

A dark passage opens, a gateway of fear,
as if to the Kingdom of Shadows,
but through it the fruit-laden orchards appear
and spring flowers grow on the meadows.
From life's heavy trials and infinite woe
I long to escape to this valley below.

From hidden springs the waters are hurled:
four rivers stream down from the crest;
they flow toward all the four streets of the world,
to the east, north, south, and the west.

With the fury and speed of their turbulent birth
they flee from the mountain to water the earth.

In the blue of the sky two pinnacles raise
their peaks over meadows and waters,
and on them, veiled with a golden haze,
dance the clouds, the celestial daughters.
They dance high above in that atmosphere chill;
no human can join in their lonely quadrille.

The queen is sitting so high and clear
on a changeless, ageless throne;
she wreathes her forehead from year to year
with many a precious stone.
The warm sun assails her with shafts of gold
which gild her but leave her still icy and cold.

Tr. J. W. Thomas

AUGUST WILHELM SCHLEGEL

(1767–1845)

THE SONNET
(DAS SONETT)

I bid: two rhymes fourfold recur,
I place them, separate, in equal lines,
That here and there two with two entwines,
And up and down they float without demur.
Harmonic's chain then two links slips
In free exchange, and each of them is three.
In such an order, such numbers do, methinks,
Make songs as subtle and as proud can be.

No laurels though for anyone who deems
My lines mere artifice and folderols,
And writes off rules as playful filigree.
But he who shares the magic of my goals
I give him height and breadth in equal teams,
And perfect balance of the rival three.

EVENING SONG FOR THE DISTANT BELOVED
(ABENDLIED FÜR DIE ENTFERNTE)

Gaze out, eyes, gaze out to the valley!
There abundant life still dwells.
Refresh yourself there in the moonlight,
And in the sacred peace.
Listen, heart, now undisturbed,
Listen to the soft sounds
That press upon you, as from afar,
For joy and for sorrow.

They teem in so wondrously,
They arouse all my longing.
This intimation, is it real?
Or is it a vain illusion?
Will my eyes one day smile in pure pleasure,
As they do now in tears?
Will blessed peace one day
Caress my heart, so often incensed?

When presentiment and memory
Are joined before our eyes,
Then at twilight
The soul's deepest shadows grow softer.
Ah, if we could not
Interweave reality with dreams,

How poor you would be, human life,
In colour, lustre and light!

Thus the heart remains constant, hoping faithfully
Unto the grave;
With love it embraces the present,
And deems itself rich in possessions.
The possessions which it creates itself
No fate can snatch from it.
It lives and works in warmth and strength,
Through trust and faith.

And if all around lies dead
In night and mist,
This heart has long ago won
A shield for every battle.
In adversity it endures its fate
With lofty defiance.
And so I fall asleep, so I awake,
If not in joy, yet in peace.

FRIEDRICH HÖLDERLIN

(1770–1843)

IN THE MORNING
(DES MORGENS)

With dew the lawn is glistening; more nimbly now,
   Awake, the stream speeds onward; the beech inclines
      Her limber head and in the leaves a
         Rustle, a glitter begins; and round the

Grey cloud-banks there a flicker of reddish flames,
   Prophetic ones, flares up and in silence plays;
      Like breakers by the shore they billow
         Higher and higher, the ever-changing.

Now come, O come, and not too impatiently,
   You golden day, speed on to the peaks of heaven!
      For more familiar and more open,
         Glad one, my vision flies up towards you

While youthful in your beauty you gaze and have
   Not grown too glorious, dazzling and proud for me;
      Speed as you will, I'd say, if only
         I could go with you, divinely ranging!

But at my happy arrogance now you smile,
   That would be like you; rather, then, rambler, bless
      My mortal acts, and this day also,
         Kindly one, brighten my quiet pathway.

from BREAD AND WINE
(BROD UND WEIN)
To Heinse

I
Round us the town is at rest; the street, in pale
    lamplight, falls quiet
  And, their torches ablaze, coaches rush through
    and away.
People go home to rest, replete with the day and its
    pleasures,
  There to weigh up in their heads, pensive, the gain
    and the loss,
Finding the balance good; stripped bare now of
    grapes and of flowers,
  As of their handmade goods, quiet the market
    stalls lie.
But faint music of strings comes drifting from
    gardens; it could be
  Someone in love who plays there, could be a man all
    alone
Thinking of distant friends, the days of his youth; and
    the fountains,
  Ever welling and new, plash amid balm-breathing
    beds.

Church bells ring; every stroke hangs still in the
    quivering half-light
  And the watchman calls out, mindful, no less, of the
    hour.
Now a breeze rises too and ruffles the crests of the
    coppice,
  Look, and in secret our globe's shadowy image, the
    moon,
Slowly is rising too; and Night, the fantastical,
    comes now
  Full of stars and, I think, little concerned about us,
Night, the astonishing, there, the stranger to all that
    is human,
  Over the mountain-tops mournful and gleaming
    draws on.

GANYMEDE
(GANYMED)

The boy sleeps, the familiar of mountains, why?
   Dull, at odds, freezing on the bare bank.
      Has he forgotten the grace he had
         At Heaven's tables, when they were thirsty?

Down here he seems not to recognise the angels
   Nor the airs playing more sharply among the rocks
     And the word a travelled man sends him,
       The old breathing word, does it never arrive?

Oh, *now* it sounds! It strikes in him like water
   Deep, coming up, as once before high among
     The rocks, sleeping, and now in a rage
       He cleanses himself of the shackles now

Now races, who seemed slow, and sloughs off the
     dross,
   Takes, breaks and casts them broken aside
     Happy with rage, so easy, on either
       Staring bank, and at this stranger's

Own voice the flocks leap to their feet, the woods
   Move and deep in the land, distant, the river's
     Being is heard and the spirit again
       Shudders to life in the navel of the earth.

The spring. And everything after its fashion
    Flowers. But he is not with us now, he went
        Away, he wandered, for they were all
            Too kind, again he speaks heavenly language.

THE HALF OF LIFE
(HÄLFTE DES LEBENS)

With yellow pears the country,
Brimming with wild roses,
Hangs into the lake,
You gracious swans,
And drunk with kisses
Your heads you dip
Into the holy lucid water.

Where, ah where shall I find,
When winter comes, the flowers,
And where the sunshine
And shadows of the earth?
Walls stand
Speechless and cold, in the wind
The weathervanes clatter.

REMEMBRANCE
(ANDENKEN)

The northeaster is blowing,
Of all winds the one I love
Best, for it promises
Fiery spirit and a good voyage
For seafarers. So go now and greet
The beautiful Garonne
And the gardens of Bordeaux,
Where on the sharp
Riverbank the path
Descends, and deep down
Into the river the brook
Cascades, but
A noble brace of oaks overlooks it,
And silver poplars;

This I do recall and how
With broad crests the elmwood
Arches over the mill,
But in the courtyard grows a figtree.
There on holidays
Brown women walk
On silken ground,
When March has come
And day and night are equal,
And over slow footpaths,

Weighted with golden dreams,
The lulling breezes move.

　　But hand me,
Someone, the fragrant cup
Brimming with dark light, that I
May rest; sleep
Would be sweet, in the shadows.
It is not good
To let mortal thoughts
Drain the soul. But conversation
Is good, and to speak
From the heart, to hear tell
Much about days of love
And deeds that have been done.

　　But where are my friends, Bellarmin
With his companion? Some hesitate
To approach the source;
For it is in the sea
That plenitude begins. They,
Like painters, compose
The beauty that is of earth, and do not shun
Winged war and a life
Years on end alone before the unleafed mast,
Where no town festivals
Make luminous the night,
Nor music, nor native dancing.

But now to the Indians
The men have gone,
There by the windy point,
By grape-clustering hills, down which
The Dordogne comes, and outward
With the glorious Garonne
Seawide the waters roll. Yet it takes away
Memory, and gives it, the sea does;
Sedulously, too, love steadies the gaze;
What abides, even then, the poets ordain it.

THE ISTER
(DER ISTER)

Come now, fire,
For we are ravenous
To see the day
And when the proof
Has flung us to our knees
We may hear the forests in uproar.
We have sung our way from the Indus
A long way and
From the Alpheus, we have searched
Years for what would serve.
Lacking wings
No one can reach across
Straight to the next
And come to the other side.
But here we shall build.
For rivers dig up
The land. And when things grow
By them and beasts go down
To them in summer to drink
So people may.

They call this river the Ister.
His course is beautiful. The columns' foliage
Burns and moves. They stand upright
In the wilds, together; and over them,

A second measure, the roof
Juts from the rocks. Which is why
The Ister invited Heracles
Who shone on Olympus
Far off and came
From the hot Isthmus
Looking for shade. Down there
They were full of fire but for the head
Coolness is needed too, so he came here
To these sources of water
And tawny banks
And the high scents and the blackness
Of fir-forests where in the depths
A hunter strolls
At noon and growth is audible
In the Ister's resinous trees.

   But he seems almost
Reversing and
Must come, I think,
From the East
And much
Might be said about that. And why
Does he cling to the hills so? The other,
The Rhine, went off
Sideways. Never for nothing
Do rivers run in the drylands. Then for what?
    To be a sign,

Nothing else, a forthright sign, and carry the sun
And moon inseparably in mind
And continue by day and by night and keep
The gods warm together.
That is why rivers
Delight the Almighty too. How else
Could he come down? And the earth's green places
They are the children of Heaven. But he,
The Ister, seems too patient,
Unfree, almost derisive. For when

   The day should start
In his youth, when he begins
To grow, when the other there
Pushes his pride high and grinds the bit
Like a colt and the air
For miles hears his tumult
This one contents himself;
But rock needs gashes
And the earth furrows
Or how should we plant and dwell?
But what that river is up to
Nobody knows.

SOPHIE MEREAU

(1770–1806)

SPRING
(FRÜHLING)

Fragrancies abound, a myriad voices
Carol in the air to left and right,
Newly young, all creaturedom rejoices,
Floating in an ocean of delight.

What resplendency, what light effuses
From vivacious Nature's glow of pride!
Festive shines the ether and encloses
All the land, as groom embraces bride.

Life flows out from all emblossomed branches,
Stirs in hiding under swamp and heath,
Dungeons forth where barren highland blanches,
Making do with rock and sand beneath.

What a lovely sparkle is outdoing
That fresh grove abloom in rosy haze!
And on mountains, ancient walls in ruin,
Falls alike its blithe and playful gaze.

There, on slender feet of silver gleaming,
Bows and waves the birches' tender green,
And their light and lissom twigs are streaming
Gaily down the zephyr's warming stream.

Dropped into a sea of sweet sensation,
Roves the soul in wondering content,
And sustained by joyous divination,
Plunges in a whirl of sentiment.

Love is who refashioned all these creatures,
His divineness shines upon me too,
And a bounteous springtime newly reaches
For my soul – foreboding told it true.

Let me sink to your maternal bosom,
Holy earth, oh my creatrix, do!
Let me feast upon your living fulness
And rejoice that I am sprung from you!

All that lives and stirs on this great ball,
All these trees, all that adorns this earth:
One dear mother's children are we all,
Children of eternal Nature's birth.

Do we not salute a single sire?
And the spirit that perfused their round,
Did it not raise up my own heart higher,
Not reverberate in my lyre's sound?

What allies me to their joys, so nearly
That by some miraculous decree
My own bosom shares in them sincerely,
Is, I feel it, sacred sympathy!

Silent! Silent! Lest the mind dismiss,
Coldly reasoning, this fair alliance!
Dare dissolve entire in love and bliss,
Rapturous heart, and offer no defiance.

TO A TRELLISED TREE
(AN EINEN BAUM AM SPALIER)

Wretched trellised tree! For, tethered tightly
To your chilly wall, you languish there,
Scarcely conscious of the zephyr's resting lightly
In the foliage of untrammeled trees,
But bypassing yours with careless ease.
Oh! The sight of you is hard to bear!
And imagination, image-bright,
By its airy magic brings the plight
Of a human shape before my gaze,
Who, forever severed from the liberal ways
Of nature, is coerced by alien norms,
Just as you are, into rigid forms.

FRIEDRICH VON HARDENBERG
('NOVALIS')
(1772–1801)

SACRED SONGS
(GEISTLICHE LIEDER)

X. THERE COME SUCH TROUBLED HOURS
(ES GIBT SO BANGE ZEITEN)

There come such troubled hours,
So heavy grows our cheer,
When all from far o'erpowers
Our hearts with ghostly fear.

There come wild terrors creeping
With stealthy silent tread,
And night's dark mantle sweeping
O'erweighs the soul with dread.

Our pillars strong are shaking,
No hold remaineth sure,
Our thoughts in whirlpools breaking
Obey our will no more.

Then madness comes and claims us
And none withstands his will,
A senses' dullness maims us,
The pulse of life stands still.

Who raised the Cross, bestowing
A refuge for each heart?
Who lives in heaven all-knowing
And healeth pain and smart?

Go thou where stands that Wonder
And to thy heart give ear.
His flames shall force asunder
And quell thy nightmare fear.

An angel bendeth o'er thee
And bears thee to the strand,
And, filled with joy, before thee
Thou seest the Promised Land.

XV. MARIA
(ICH SEHE DICH IN TAUSEND BILDERN)

A thousand portraits strive to render
your face and form with loving art,
but none, Maria, is so tender
as that I painted in my heart.

The tumults of the world have faded
since then, and blown as empty dreams,
and heaven's sweetness has pervaded
my soul in everlasting streams.

HYMNS TO NIGHT
(HYMNEN AN DIE NACHT)

II.

Must morning always return? Will the might of the earthly never end? Accursed busy-ness consumes Night's heavenly touch. Will Love's secret sacrifice never burn forever? Light's days are measured; but timeless and spaceless is the reign of Night – Eternal is the duration of Sleep. Holy Sleep – bless not too seldom in their daily tasks those consecrated to Night. Only fools fail to recognize you and know no other sleep than the shadow you mercifully cast over us in that dusk of the true Night. They do not sense you in the grape's golden flood – in the almond tree's miraculous oil, in the brown juice of the poppy. They do not realize that it is you who hover about the bosom of the tender maiden and make a heaven of her womb – they have no inkling that it is you who comes to meet us in ancient tales, opening the heavens and bearing the keys to the dwellings of the blest, silent messenger of infinite mysteries.

VI. LONGING FOR DEATH
(SEHNSUCHT NACH DEM TODE)

Now down into the womb of earth,
Away from this Light's kingdom,
Our raging pain and sense of dearth
But hail a new dominion;
And sailing in our narrow bark
We'll soon the shores of heaven mark.

Let us now praise eternal Night,
And praise eternal slumber.
The heat of day has sapped our might,
Long sorrows without number.
To dwell abroad has lost its charms,
We long for home, our Father's arms.

What good to us a world like this?
What hope of true Love's sharing?
What was of yore is now dismissed,
The new leaves us uncaring.
Oh, sad and lonely evermore
Whose heart is with the days of yore!

The days of yore, when senses bright
In highest flame were burning,
And mankind still was sound of sight,
God's face and hand discerning;

Then lofty mind and simple heart
Still many with God's image marked.

The days of yore, when ancient clans
In fullest bloom still flourished,
And children, to gain heaven's strand,
The hope of torment nourished.
Though worldly joy and life still spake,
Full many a heart for Love did break.

The days of yore, when God himself
In prime of youth descended,
And out of Love his blessèd self
To early death commended;
And from him drove not fear and pain
That ours might be the dearer gain.

With yearning sick those times we see
In darkest Night concealèd.
This realm of time we sure must flee
Ere our pain can be healèd.
We must our way straight homeward wend
To see those holy times again.

What still impedes our swift return?
Our loved ones long are resting.
Their grave is our own mortal bourn,
Our fears grow more distressing.

We've nothing more to look for here –
The heart is full – the world is sere.

In infinite and secret wise
A thrill of awe steals through us –
I think I heard from distant skies
An echo of our sadness.
Our loved ones must feel longing too –
Their longing keeps our longing true.

So down then to the blessèd bride,
To Jesus, the belovèd,
Take comfort, evening shades abide
About his grieving lovers.
A dream will break our bonds apart
And sink us in the Father's heart.

THE HERMIT'S SONG
(GERN VERWEIL ICH NOCH IM TALE)
from *Heinrich von Ofterdingen*

Here I linger still with pleasure,
smiling in the deepest night,
since love's overflowing measure
comes to me with morning's light.

By these holy drops exalted
now my soul can boldly soar,
in this life, till I have vaulted
drunkenly to heaven's door.

I am lulled in blissful seeing
till all pain and fears depart.
O! The queen of every being
gives to me her faithful heart.

Bitter years of tears have broken
and transformed this clay for me,
and engraved thereon a token,
granting it eternity.

But those days that know no number
seem no longer than a breath;
when my life sinks into slumber
I'll give thanks for them in death.

FRIEDRICH SCHLEGEL

(1772–1829)

THE BOATMAN
(DER SCHIFFER)

Peacefully I lie stretched out,
Turning the rudder this way and that,
Breathing the cool air in the moonlight,
Tranquil in spirit, dreaming sweetly.
And I let the boat drift,
Gazing into the shining waters,
Where the stars shimmer enchantingly;
And again I play with the rudder.

If only that fair-haired girl
Were reclining on the seat before me,
Singing tenderly soulful songs,
Then I should feel blissfully happy.
I should let the child tease me
And flirt again with the sweet girl.

Peacefully I lie stretched out,
Tranquil in spirit, dreaming sweetly,
Breathing the cool air in the moonlight,
Moving the rudder this way and that.

SUNSET
(ABENDRÖTE)

The sun sinks deeper,
All things breathe peace;
The day's work is finished
And the children play merrily.
The green earth shines greener
Before the sun goes down.
The flowers softly breathe
Into the air sweet balm
That tenderly caresses the soul
While the senses are drunk with rapture.
Small birds, people in the distance,
Mountains soaring heavenwards,
And the great silver river
That winds its slender course through the valley:
All seem to speak to the poet,
For he has divined their meaning;
And the whole world becomes a single choir,
Singing many a song with one voice.

LUDWIG TIECK

(1773–1853)

SWEET DARLING, REST IN THE SHADE
(SCHLAFLIED)

Sweet darling, rest in the shade
of this green, translucent night;
the grass soughs in the meadows,
the leaves fan you and cool you,
and faithful love watches.
Sleep, sleep,
the woods rustle more softly,
I am yours for ever.

Be still, you hidden songsters,
and do not disturb her sweet rest.
The thronging birds listen,
their loud song is hushed –
my darling, close your eyes.
Sleep, sleep
in the twilight
I will guard you.

Whisper your harmonious song,
sing on, gentle brook;
beautiful thoughts of love
speak through these melodies,
gentle dreams follow.
Through the murmuring grove
golden bees swarm
and hum you to sleep.

WONDER OF LOVE
(WUNDER DER LIEBE)

Magic night of shining moonbeams,
Night that holds the mind in thrall.
Wondrous magic world apart.
Then splendour rises, only hear!

Love, you have to seek it, glimpse it,
Never learned, it no-one teaches.
Who the flame would set alight
And the fire his whole self reaches
Must wash off the sins that blight.
He stays wake: the whole world dreams,
From love's star the laughter gleams,
Golden eyes him then behold
And he sees the charm unfold,
Magic night of shining moonbeams.

Never, though, must he take fright
When the clouds come scudding darkly,
Darkness covers bright stars' light
And the moon is willing hardly
To shed a shimmer to our sight.
Ever stands the tent of love,
Lit within, its own bright wall.
Only boldness here can break

What in fear is left to quake.
Night that holds the mind in thrall.

Love, mark, will not find its way
To a soul that's in dejection.
Fleeting hours the golden ray,
But for him it is rejection
With his long face all the day.
Hold the serpent to your heart
Then the shadows are your part.
What the poets say of yore
He calls, poor wretch, ever more
Wondrous magic world apart.

Heart aloft in faithful flower
Feels anon the golden rays,
Grace and love, its inward bower,
Self and others it embays.
Flames sweet burn its inward dower.
Once you make your votive prayer,
To the heavens you must bear
If once love has seized your souls
On its altar's fiery coals.
Then splendour rises, only hear!

Tr. Roger Paulin

LOVE
(LIEBE)

Love must think in music sweetly,
for all thought is too remote.
Only music can denote
all that love desires completely.
Love we know and know her only
when the voice of music sounds;
while her magic still abounds,
love can never leave us lonely.
Love would die a sterile death,
did not music lend her breath.

CLEMENS BRENTANO

(1778–1842)

SLUMBER SONG
(WIEGENLIED)

Softly, softly, sing a tune;
Sing a whispered lullaby;
Learn thy lay from Lady Moon,
Moving soundless through the sky.

Sing a song as sweetly sighing
As the springs on pebbles curling,
As the bees round linden flying
Humming, trickling, rustling, purling.

EVENING SERENADE
(ABENDSTÄNDCHEN)

Hear the flute's bewailing sound,
see the noisy fountains glisten,
golden notes are all around,
silence, silence, let us listen!

Gentle pleading, tender longing,
how it sweetly speaks to me!
Through night's shadows, darkly thronging,
gleams the light of melody.

LORE LAY
(LORE LAY)

At Bacharach on Rhine-bank
A sorceress did dwell,
She was so fine and handsome
On all she cast her spell.

Full many a man around her
To grievous shame she brought;
No more could he be rescued
Who in her toils was caught.

The bishop sent to bid her
Before his court appear;
Yet must he grant her pardon
She was so passing fair.

He spoke to her with tremors,
'Thou poor young Lore Lay,
Who then has thus misled thee
To evil sorcery?'

'Lord Bishop, let me perish,
I'm weary now to live,
For all that look upon me
Alas, must come to grief.

Thy eyes like flames are burning
My arm's a magic staff,
O lay me in the burning,
O break for me my staff!'

'I cannot yet condemn thee
Till thou hast made me know
Why in thine eyes so burning
My heart begins to glow?

The staff I cannot shatter,
Thou Lore Lay so fine,
For then I have to sever
In twain this heart of mine.'

'Lord Bishop, to poor maiden
Show not such cruel scorn:
But beg that God have mercy
On maiden so forlorn.

I dare to live no longer;
I love none any more;
Death is what you must give me,
For that is why I'm here.

My lover hath betrayed me,
From me hath turned away,

Gone forth on distant journey
In foreign land doth stray.

Eyes that are wild and timid,
The red and white in cheeks,
Words sounding quiet and gentle,
My magic circle makes.

Me too it brings to ruin,
My heart is woe in me,
For sadness would I perish
When I my likeness see.

Then let my judgment find me,
As Christian let me die;
For everything is empty
Since he's no longer by.'

He had three knights brought thither:
'To convent take her hence.'
'Go Lore! In God's keeping
Be thy distracted sense!

Thou now shalt be a novice,
In black and white a nun;
On earth thou shalt prepare thee
For when life's days are done!'

To convent now they're riding,
All three the knights go by,
And sadly in the middle
The lovely Lore Lay.

'O knights, I pray you let me
Climb this great rocky hill,
Once more I'd see the castle,
Where my dear love did dwell.

Once more to look I'm longing
Into the deep Rhine flood,
Then will I to the convent
And virgin be of God.'

So steep the rock was standing,
Precipitous its face,
Yet climbed she to the summit
And stood at topmost place.

Their steeds the three knights tethered
And made them fast beneath,
Then up above they clambered
And rocky summit reached.

Then said the maid: 'There journeys
A little skip on Rhine

The one who stands on shipboard
Must be that love of mine!

It must be my beloved
So blithe my heart doth grow.'
Then leaned she down and over
And plunged to depths below.

Nor could the knights from summit
Descend their lives to save,
Up there they all must perish,
With neither priest nor grave.

And who has sung this ditty?
A boatman on the Rhine,
And ever has the echo
Come from the Three-Knights-Stone:
       Lore Lay!
       Lore Lay!
       Lore Lay!
As were the three my own.

THE SPINSTRESS' SONG
(DER SPINNERIN LIED)

Of yore, as now, aringing
Sweet sang the nightingale.
We heard the echo trail,
Each to the other clinging.

I sing to keep from weeping
And spin, all lonesome here,
The thread so pure and clear
Until the moon sets, sleeping.

Each to the other clinging
We heard the nightingale.
But now the echoes trail,
For you did leave me, singing.

Ere yet the moon sets sleeping,
My thoughts roam far from here.
My heart is pure and clear.
God join us in His keeping.

Since you did leave me, singing,
I hear the nightingale.
We heard the echoes trail,
Faintly together clinging.

God join us in His keeping.
I spin, all lonesome here,
The moon shines pure and clear,
I sing and would be weeping.

THE FOREST
(O KÜHLER WALD)

O forest fair
where do you sigh,
in which my darling plays?
O echo rare,
where do you lie,
that listens to my lays?

O echo, stay
and sing to her
the dreams which I have strewn.
My every lay
O bring to her,
whom I have lost so soon.

My heart is where
the forest weeps
in which my darling plays.
And, troubled, there
the echo sleeps,
and scattered are my lays.

So lonely are
the forest ways;
O love, come wander too.
Though scattered far
my many lays,
I've more to sing to you.

LORD! WITHIN THY PEACE I REST ME
(HERR! ICH STEH IN DEINEM FRIEDEN)

Lord! Within thy peace I rest me,
Whether life or death I merit;
Here below my Savior perished
That I may his grace inherit.

Longs the butterfly for sunlight
It must break its woven mansion;
So art thou this house destroying
That my freedom find expansion.

Such a death I pray thou grant me,
Lord! when life has reached its reaping,
Grant that, senses clear, I give my
Soul again within thy keeping!

For within thy hands are lying
Hearts with humble meekness glowing
Like the infant in the cradle
Tranquil sleeping, grief unknowing!

HOLY NIGHT, HOLY NIGHT!
(HEIL'GE NACHT, HEIL'GE NACHT!)

Holy night, holy night!
Star-made peace of heav'nly wonder,
All that light has torn asunder
One and bound now
And all wounds now
Sweetly bleed in evening's red.

Bjelbog's spear, Bjelbog's spear,
Drunken earth's heart penetrating,
Earth with blissful celebrating,
Rose aglow,
In lust's tow,
Sinks within the womb of dark.

Modest bride, modest bride!
Your sweet shame must now surrender
When the wedding cup is tendered
Brimming over!
Thus brims over
Into ardent night the day.

ECHOES OF BEETHOVEN'S MUSIC
(NACHKLÄNGE BEETHOVENSCHER MUSIK)

I

Sacred mother of deep springs,
Solitude, oh silent well,
Mirror of the inner suns
Which, imaged, into music swell.
Since the time when I put down
My errors on your blissful path,
Since the time I wholly drowned
Within your dark and wondrous bath,
I am endued in glitter's gown.
For what rings bright in me, the staff
Of a god may count the beat and bars,
A soul's song of circling stars.
The suns that in my heart have shone,
The planets that my rapture share,
The comets that my anguish own,
Play in my breast their full-toned air.
In my melancholy's moon,
Of every splendor unaware,
Humble I must sing out my tune
At treasures hidden deep within me,
At hardships where my life is caught,
At peaks for which my quest has sought,
And, eternal God, recall Thee!
All else would be done for naught.

II

Oh God, hair-seized, your heaven lifts me high,
And yet your earth to hell must drag me down,
Oh Lord, in what cache shall my heart abide,
That I may sure and safe your threshold own?
Thus I pray hot throughout the night, my cries
Flow ceaseless like a fire-well's burning band,
And make me captive, caught in flaming seas,
And yet, among them, I've a place to stand,
Like unto cryptic giant forms I rise,
A Memnon's statue: morning's first suns send
Their querying beams as arrows at my mind,
And dreams which from the midnight's loom descend
I weave to greet the day in music's kind.

III

Blessed the man who, senses shorn,
Hovers like a spirit over the waters.
And shifts not flags with time
As a ship does, unfurling
Sails to catch the winds the day may bring.
No, senses shorn likest unto God,
Knowing but himself, creating,
He makes the world that he himself is,
And mankind sins upon it,
And it was not his will!
Yet all is divided.
No one is vouchsafed all, for each thing

Has a lord set to it, save the Lord;
Alone He stands, and serves not.
Thus, too, the singer.

Tr. George. C. Schoolfield

KAROLINE VON GÜNDERRODE

(1780–1806)

THE KISS IN THE DREAM
(DER KUSS IM TRAUME)

The breath of life was brought me by a kiss,
It quieted my bosom's deepest grief.
Come, Darkness, wrap me close in night's relief,
That my dry lips may drink in my new bliss.

In dreams my life was all suffused with calm,
And so I live to contemplate my dreams;
I scorn all other joys, for all their gleams,
For only night can breathe out such sweet balm.

Love's sweetest joys the day restrains for spite,
He hurts me with his vain and gaudy light,
His sun consumes me with its scorching fires.

So hide yourself, Eye, from its earthly beams!
Conceal yourself in night, it quiets your desires
And heals your hurt, like Lethe's cooling streams.

DEDICATION
(ZUEIGNUNG)

In grave, quiet hours, in blessed solitude,
I wove this wreath, in contemplation deep,
Flowers of the present and of time's great keep:
These blooms of mine, a garland now for you.

You, I know, that message will receive,
Enclosed within each flower's petals furled,
The quiet spirit, concealed still from the world,
Which the consecrated eye alone perceives.

And so too girls in Eastern lands their wreath
Of many colours weave; in search of praise
The blooms compete, their little faces raised.

Yet the adept looks beyond that outer sheath,
Those signs and symbols knowingly observes;
With him in turn they silently converse.

THE PRIME LAMENT
(DIE EINE KLAGE)

Whom in soul and mind oppresses
The profoundest of distresses,
Parting's bitter smart,
Who had cherished what was taken,
By his dearest was forsaken:
The beloved heart,

Tastes within delight the burning
Tears, and love's perennial yearning
To be one in twain,
Find in one the other ever,
Thus the bounds of self to sever
And all being's pain.

Who with all her heart and nature
Came to love a human creature
Ah! is not consoled
By the thought that joys departed
Usher in some newly started –
They can't match the old.

That sweet state of living, learning
Both accepting and returning
Words and looks and airs,
Eager search and joyous ending,
Sentiment and apprehending,
Not a god repairs.

BRIGHT RED
(HOCHROTH)

You deepest red,
Till I am dead
My love shall be like you,
Nor shall it fade,
Till I am dead,
You glowing red,
My love shall be like you.

THE BALLOONIST
(DER LUFTSCHIFFER)

Upon the great blue ocean
That flows around the shining stars,
I have travelled in a rocking boat
And met the heavenly powers.
I've been lost in contemplation,
Escaping from all earthly things,
And drunk the ether of eternity;
I've known the writing of the stars
And in their cycles and their rings
Seen an image of the sacred cadence
That mightily draws every sound
Into the surging force of harmony.
But alas! I am pulled down,
My view the mist enshrouds,
The bounds of earth I see again,
And am driven back by clouds.
Woe! Gravity's stern law
Reasserts its case:
No one may withdraw
From the earthbound race.

ADALBERT VON CHAMISSO

(1781–1838)

THE SOLDIER
(DER SOLDAT)

To muffled drums we move along.
Still far the spot. The way how long!
O were he at rest, and the whole thing through!
I believe my heart will break in two.

In all the world I've loved but him,
Who now must meet a death so grim.
The squad forms up to a martial air;
And I, with the rest, am paraded there.

Now for the last time dwells his gaze
Upon the sunlight's God-sent rays.
Then round his eyes a cloth they tied. –
God's peace eternal with you bide!

The nine take aim in order due.
Eight bullets past him harmless flew;
    – They all were quaking with anguish dread –
But through his heart my bullet sped.

Tr. Geoffrey Herbert Chase

LORD BYRON'S LAST LOVE
(LORD BYRONS LETZTE LIEBE)

Byron has arrived! The brightest pupil
Of Ares and the Muses is revealed:
Hero among Hellas' heroic sons
On freedom's blood-fertilized field.

The hearts of all the Greeks now beat for him –
All hearts but one, though for that one he yearns;
While he brings salvation to the people
In unrelenting grief himself he burns.

'As my people do, so will I revere you!'
Mild but unmoved does the maiden speak:
'Byzantium's crown you may covet,
Only my love you are not to seek!'

Urgently once he was summoned to her
Who is the star of his inner night;
Full of dread he followed the messenger. –
He stood before a picture of fright!

Rigid, motionless, she lay in grief,
A sword held tightly in her right hand;
The splendid figure, pale and spiritlike,
Lifts her head and brings herself to stand,

And begins: 'There is something you must know.
When I was young my heart made its choice,
And to my palikar I gave his sword
Obedient to my country's voice.

Parting, I was earnest at an earnest hour:
"Only victory or death, we know;
Up then! and one word from faithful lips:
If you die for our people, I die for you."

Now you see me dying for the dead one;
The sword he sent me falling you inherit;
Take this sacred gift, O poet hero! –
Worthy of me only as you bear it.'

He examines it with horror. Calmly
She speaks, 'Poison!' – breathes out scarcely a breath,
And it is done; – his arms first embrace
The dream of his life at her death.

Byron's features since that hour like his fate
Were bleak and overcast with nightlike gloom;
And soon he took the palikar's sword
With him to the bosom of the tomb.

JUSTINUS KERNER

(1786–1862)

OPPRESSIVE DREAM
(DER SCHWERE TRAUM [IKAROS])

I dreamt I flew all fearful
Into the world afar,
To Strassburg through the side-streets,
Before my sweetheart's door.

Sweetheart is so saddened,
My flying makes her cry:
'It was the Evil Spirit
Who taught you how to fly!'

Now Sweetheart, what use lying,
Since you know all full well,
The one who taught me flying,
It was the Fiend from Hell!

And Sweetheart weeps, a-crying
And wakes me with her cry,
And here, alas! in Augsburg
A prisoner I lie.

Tomorrow I'll be hanging,
No Sweetheart calls to me,
Tomorrow I'll be soaring,
A bird in the air and free.

Tr. John Fitzell

THE SAW-MILL
(DER WANDRER IN DER SÄGEMÜHLE)

Down there beside the saw-mill
  In sweet repose I lay,
And watched the waters speeding
  The saw-wheel's roundelay.

And watched the blade bright-gleaming,
  And felt like one who dreams,
As through the fir-tree's body
  It cut long, furrowed seams.

The fir, as if still living,
  Through all its fibres shook;
And in its high-pitched anguish,
  These mournful words it spoke:

'Full well the hour you've chosen,
  O wanderer, here to stray;
It is for you I suffer
  These wounds my heart that flay.

It is for you, when, fleeting,
  Your roaming days are o'er,
This wood a chest will fashion
  To rest in evermore.'

Four planks I then saw falling.
  I felt my heart go chill.
A word I sought to stammer;
  But now the wheels were still.

LUDWIG UHLAND

(1787–1862)

THE CHAPEL
(DIE KAPELLE)

O'erlooking calm the vale below
   The Chapel crowns the hill;
Beneath glad songs the shepherd boy
   Sings by the meadow rill.

Sad tolls the bell, and solemn hymn
   Their dirge the funeral train;
The boy hath hush'd his carol gay,
   And lists the mournful strain.

There they who in the vale rejoiced,
   Unto the grave they bring;
There too, thou blythesome shepherd boy,
   To thee they'll one day sing!

Tr. Charles K. Lambert

THE DREAM
(DER TRAUM)

Two lovers in a garden fair
Stray'd hand in hand along,
Two pallid and two sickly forms,
They sat the flow'rs among.

They kiss'd each other on the cheek,
Each other on the mouth,
In firm embrace each other held,
Health came again and youth.

Two bells rung forth their matin peal,
Straight pass'd the dream away;
She lonely in the cloister's cell,
He deep in dungeon lay.

THE SMITH
(DER SCHMIED)

My sweetheart is there;
his hammer is swinging,
the roaring and ringing,
the echoes and swells
resound as of bells
through alleys and square.

My lover sits where
the furnace is nigh him,
and when I walk by him
the bellows will blow,
the embers will glow
and flames fill the air.

SPRING FAITH
(FRÜHLINGSGLAUBE)

The winds again are mild and light;
they whisper and wander day and night,
through field and forest wending.
O fresh perfume, O youthful sound,
now, wretched heart, be thou unbound!
For now must all the world be mending.

The earth grows lovelier day by day;
what yet may be, no one can say:
the blossoming seems unending.
The farthest, deepest valley flowers;
now, heart, forget the painful hours,
for now must all the world be mending.

THE GOSSAMER
(DER SOMMERFADEN)

There flies, as through the fields we rove,
A Gossamer across the land,
Frail web of light by Fairies wove,
And ties from me to her a band.
I take it for a favouring sign,
I hold it as Love's needed token –
O hopes that for the sanguine shine,
Of vapour spun, by zephyr broken!

ON THE DEATH OF A CHILD
(AUF DEN TOD EINES KINDES)

You came, you went, a fleeting guest
Upon the earth you lightly trod.
From where to where? We only know:
From God into the hands of God.

JOSEPH FREIHERR VON EICHENDORFF

(1788–1857)

THE BROKEN RING
(DAS ZERBROCHENE RINGLEIN)

Beside the shaded water
an ancient mill wheel turns,
but now the miller's daughter
has left those rocks and ferns.

She gave a ring, a token
of pledges to be true;
her promises were broken,
my ring then broke in two.

I would as minstrel wander
the wide world up and down,
and sing my songs out yonder
from town to distant town!

I would with gallant squires
ride to the bloody fight,
and sleep by silent fires
upon the field at night!

I hear the mill wheel turning
and know not what I will.
For death I'm ever longing,
for then it would be still.

Tr. J. W. Thomas

DIALOGUE IN THE FOREST
(WALDGESPRÄCH)

'The hour is late, the sun is gone.
Why are you riding here alone?
The woodland's wide, I'll be your guide
And lead you home, my lovely bride!'

'Men's falseness and deceit are great;
Crushed is my heart beneath grief's weight.
The hunting horn sounds far and near –
Oh flee if life you cherish dear!'

'Your splendid steed, your dazzling dress,
Your body's young seductiveness –
I know you now! God hear my cry!
You are the sorceress Lorelei!'

'You know me well – a castle's mine
That towers high above the Rhine.
The hour is late, chill grows the eve.
This forest you shall never leave!'

THE JOYFUL TRAVELLER
(DER FROHE WANDERSMANN)

The man whom God will show true favor,
He ushers forth to live his dream;
He gives Him all his best to savor
In wood and hill and field and stream.

The rosy dawn can never thrill them,
Those lazy souls who lie abed.
Their lives? Why, rocking cradles fill them,
And troubles, cares, and need for bread.

The brooks go leaping down the mountain,
The larks whir high to show their art;
Why can't my song burst from the fountain
Of my full throat and happy heart?

The ruling power, to God reserve it;
The brook, the lark, the field, the wood,
The earth, the sky, He will preserve it,
And guide my life to make it good.

Tr. Stewart H. Benedict

PRAGUE STUDENTS' SONG
(WANDERLIED DER PRAGER STUDENTEN)

Southward the birds go, every wing
Taking flight together;
And here the wanderers gaily swing
Their caps in sunny weather.
Fine gentlemen and students all,
They tread the sunny highway
And on their horns they play their call,

Their taunting, scornful, wry way:
'Good-bye to Prague, we leave you now,
And face the world with cloudless brow:
"Et habeat bonam pacem
Qui sedet post fornacem."

'At night we rove the indifferent town,
The windows gleam with candles;
Beyond the glass, the party gown
And gliding dancers' sandals.
We play our tune before the door –
Which always doubles thirsting –
And through the happy portal pour
Since our dry throats are bursting.
Innkeeper, bring us each a fine
Tankard of beer, or glass of wine.

"Venit ex sua domo
Beatus ille homo!"

'At other times Boreas blows,
And leafless days are colder;
We tramp the fields through winter snows;
Each storm makes us grow older.
Our fluttering capes in rags will fall,
Our thin shoes drag on highway,
But on our horns we'll play our call,
Our taunting, scornful, wry way:
"Beatus ille homo,
Qui sedet in sua domo
Et sedet post fornacem
Et habet bonam pacem!"'

EVENING
(ABEND)

Man's noisy pleasures are at rest:
From earth a dreamlike rustle rises
Through all its trees and tantalizes
The heart with strangeness half-confessed,
Times that are gone, griefs grown weaker;
Faint shiverings are felt and flicker
Like summer lightning through the breast.

NOCTURNE
(NACHTS)

I wander through the silent night;
The moon slips secret, soft, and bright
Oft from its darkening cloudy cover.
And now along the vale
Wakens the nightingale
Till a gray hush again spreads over.

O wonder-filled nocturnal song,
Far hidden waters whisper long,
Trees shiver as the moonlight gleams –
Under the spell you cast
My wandering song is lost
And like a calling-out of dreams.

Tr. Herman Salinger

ON THE DEATH OF MY CHILD
(AUF MEINES KINDES TOD)

Far off the clocks are striking,
The night is growing late,
The lamp is burning low now,
Your little bed is made.

Only the wind is wailing
Round about the house
While we sit here lonely,
Listening without.

It is as if you were softly
Going to knock on the door,
Tired after straying,
And come back once more.

Foolish, foolish people!
We are the ones who roam
Still lost in dread of the darkness –
You have long since been home.

NIGHT
(DIE NACHTBLUME)

Night is like a silent sea,
Joy and pain and love's sad urging
Reach us so confusedly
Through the gentle wavelet's surging.

Wishes like light clouds afloat,
Through the quiet spaces drifting,
In this soft wind who can note
If they're thoughts or dream-wraiths shifting?

If I silence voice and heart,
Which would cry out vainly urging
To the stars, still deep apart
Sounds that gentle wavelets' surging.

Tr. Isabel S. MacInnes

LONGING
(SEHNSUCHT)

So golden the stars were shining.
At the window I stood alone.
Through silent fields far echoed
A posthorn's joyous tone.
My heart caught fire, inflaming
My secret thoughts' delight:
Who would not, too, go roving
On a lovely summer's night?

And down the mountain pathway
Two youths came striding by;
The songs that they were singing
Awoke the silent sky.
They sang of rustling forests,
Where gorges meet the sight,
Of torrents downward gushing
Toward the forest's night.

They sang of marble statues,
And palaces of stone,
Of gardens in the moonlight,
Their misty bowers o'ergrown;
Where maids at casements listen,
When lutes their hearts excite,
And drowsy fountains murmur
On a lovely summer's night.

NIGHT OF MOON
(MONDNACHT)

It was, as if with kisses
   The sky the earth had stilled,
Till deep in moon-lit blossoms,
   Her dreams alone he filled.

The silent corn was swaying,
   Caressed by breezes light;
The woodlands softly rustled,
   So star-clear was the night.

And taking flight, my spirit,
   Its pinions wide outspread,
Through silent spaces soaring,
   As though it homeward sped.

THE HERMIT
(DER EINSIEDLER)

Balm of the world, come, quiet night!
Thou sinkest from the mountains' height,
The evening winds are sleeping.
A sailor only, travel-worn,
Sings cross the port alone, forlorn,
His praise for God's safekeeping.

Like drifting clouds the years roll by.
Forgotten by the world stand I
Alone in all creation.
But oft thy comfort came to me
When underneath a rustling tree
I sat in contemplation.

Balm of the world, thou quiet night!
I'm wearied by the day's great might,
The wide, wide sea is darkling,
Grant me to rest from joy and woe
Till the eternal morning glow
Sets the dark forest sparkling.

WISHING WAND
(WÜNSCHELRUTE)

Slumb'ring deep in every thing
Dreams a song as yet unheard,
And the world begins to sing
If you find the magic word.

DEATH WISH
(TODESLUST)

Death-drunk the swan in waters seeks its grave,
To sink still dreaming, singing in the wave;
The summer-wearied earth, when flowers no longer
    blow,
In clustered grapes sets all her fires aglow;
The sun, still showering sparks throughout the west,
Lends earth his warmth once more before he sets,
Till, star on star, a marvel to behold,
Arises Night, the drunk earth to enfold.

MEMENTO MORI
(MEMENTO MORI!)

Eat oysters, hoard ducats
As much as you're able,
You still have to die!
Then the worms come to table
And your heirs can live high.

THE POET WALKS ABROAD
(WANDERNDER DICHTER)

I know not how it comes about:
I scarcely from my home step out,
Than suddenly a lark takes flight
And fills the blue with trilled delight.

The grass and flowers everywhere
Have pearls and jewels in their hair;
Slim poplars, shrubs, all things that grow,
In greatest state before me bow.

First with the news the brook's away;
And where wind-parted tree-tops sway,
The meadow steals a glance at me,
As if my loving bride she'd be.

When, tired, at night I'm back once more,
Lo! serenades me at my door
The nightingale; in woods around
Soon glow-worms will illume the ground.

Don't ask me why!   It just is so. –
No poet walks incognito.
He knows at once, does merry Spring,
Within his kingdom who is king.

OLD AGE
(DAS ALTER)

High with the clouds migrating birds forgather.
Earth sleeps, the boughs half stripped where foliage
    sprang.
Hushed are the songs that late so sweetly rang,
And winter covers all with gloomy weather.

The wall clock ticks, and still with ruffled feather
Softly the bird sings which in autumn sang.
You turn, shielded from ice and storm's harangue,
A picture book which holds the past together.

Often such mildness age would have me learn.
Wait: overnight the wind will turn with grace,
And you may feel from roofs the dew descending.

One at the window knocks with happy face.
Astonished, you step out, nor then return,
For the spring comes at last which has no ending.

Tr. Vernon Watkins

FRIEDRICH RÜCKERT

(1788–1866)

MY SOUL, MY HEART
(DU MEINE SEELE)

O thou my soul, O thou my heart,
thou my delight, my pain thou art,
the world art thou, which I discover,
my heaven thou, in which I hover,
O thou my grave, the open tomb
in which I bury grief and gloom!
My rest and my tranquility
art thou, that heaven granted me.
That thou shouldst love me, makes me greater,
thy glance has been my new creator,
thou raisest me with love on high,
my guiding light, my better I.

O STOP WITH ME
(DU BIST DIE RUH)

Thou art repose
and quiet calm,
desire that glows
and cooling balm.

I give thee, dear,
with joy and sighs
a dwelling here –
my heart and eyes.

Stop in with me
and be not late,
and after thee
make fast the gate.

Have care depart
from out this breast,
and fill my heart
with love, and rest.

Alone through thee
my eyes have sight:
O let them be
filled with thy light.

'NOW THE SUN PREPARES TO RISE AS BRIGHTLY'

('NUN WILL DIE SONN' SO HELL AUFGEH'N')

Now the sun prepares to rise as brightly
as if the night had brought no cause for grief.
The grief was mine alone.
The sun shines for all alike.

You must not shut the night into yourself
but drown it in eternal light.
A lamp went out in my tent –
I bless the light that gladdens all the world!

CLOSING SONG
(SCHLUSSLIED)

O fragrance which sustains my soul, do not leave me!
O dream which escorts me through life, do not
    leave me!
Thou fine bird of Paradise, which hovers close by
With wings unseen, yet rustling soft, do not leave me!
Thou art both nurse and nurs'ry rhymes from times
    long past!
Without you I am orphaned – ah, do not leave me!
You have endured, abiding with me when youth fled;
Should you flee too, then I turn grey, do not leave me;
O thou my Spring! see how autumn blows about
    me now;
Come, lest the winter freeze me in ice, do not
    leave me;
O breath of peace! hear how life rages about me now;
Who is there to give quiet counsel? Do not leave me!
O thou my frenzy! thou my love! O thou my song!
Which here, through me, exalts itself, do not leave me!

WILHELM MÜLLER

(1794–1827)

THE JOURNEYMAN'S SONG
(WANDERSCHAFT)

Oh wandering is a miller's joy,
Oh wandering!
He must a sorry miller be
Who never wanted to be free
For wandering!

The water taught us what to do,
The water!
For it rests not by night or day,
And always strains to be away,
The water!

We learn it from the millwheels too,
The millwheels!
They're like the water down below,
I've never seen them weary grow,
The millwheels!

The millstones too, though heavy they,
The millstones!
In merry circles round they dance,
Would like to faster race and prance,
The millstones!

Oh wandering, wandering, my delight,
Oh wandering!
Oh master, mistress Miller, pray
Let me in peace now go away
And wander!

THE LINDEN TREE
(DER LINDENBAUM)

Before the gateway fountain
there stands a linden tree.
Within its shadows dreaming,
such sweet dreams came to me.

I cut into its gray bark
so many a loving name –
and here in joy and sorrow
is where I always came.

Today I had to wander
right by when night was deep.
Just there once more in darkness
I closed my eyes in sleep.

And all its branches rustled,
the leaves called wistfully:
Come here to me, dear fellow,
you'll find your peace with me.

Cold blasts of wind blew sharply,
cut straight into my face.
My hat flew from my head too –
I never changed my pace.

And now the miles are many
I've wandered without cease,
And still I hear the rustling:
'Tis there that you'd find peace!

AUGUST GRAF
VON PLATEN-HALLERMÜNDE

(1797–1848)

TRUEST OF SAGES ARE YOU TO ME
(DU BIST DER WAHRE WEISE MIR)

Truest of sages are you to me,
Your eye speaks softly true to me;
A friend of friends without a mask
You walk this long march through with me;
Not life alone but living love
Is what your life has proved to me;
The fragrant musk of love you bring,
The food of truth, as due to me;
Deep in your sphere I lay, my dear,
So warm, so bright it grew to me:
I saw you as the pearl of price
Above all other good to me.

Tr. Edwin Morgan

FAIN WOULD I LIVE IN SAFEST FREEDOM
(ICH MÖCHTE GERN MICH FREI BEWAHREN)

Fain would I live in safest freedom,
Free from the world, safe from its crowds.
Fain would I walk by quiet rivers,
Roofed by a shady tent of clouds.

Flurrying wings and summer feathers
Would brush my sullen days away.
Guilt-ridden men would shun the cleanness
Of air, the embrace of purity.

A boat upon a stream, forever,
Grazing the bank but rarely, drawn
To reach a young rose, and returning
To the mid-current running on.

Watching the herds far off, at pasture,
Fresh-hearted flowers every spring,
Vinemen lopping the grape harvest,
Reapers at the heady haymaking.

For food I'd have the light of heaven,
Bright, unstained, it cannot change!
And I would drink the living wellspring,
That blood might rest, not race and range.

VENETIAN SONNETS
(SONETTE AUS VENEDIG)

II.

This labyrinth of bridges and cramped streets
Which twist and cross and mix a myriad ways,
How shall I ever master it? This maze,
How can I penetrate its far retreats?

Let me climb St. Mark's tower; the eye greets
Light and space, gazing from these terraces;
And all the great surrounding riches raise
One picture where a double grace competes.

There I salute the ocean, blue at noon;
And here the Alps, the wave that never broke,
Looming above the islanded lagoon.

See how this place drew an audacious folk:
They came, and palaces and temples soon
Rose from the very waves on props of oak.

Tr. Edwin Morgan

I love you, as the sum of all those forms
Which Venice in its paintings shows to us.
The very heart may yearn, 'Come close to us!'
But they stand silent, we pass by their charms.

I see you as the breathing stone whose arms
Hold beauty carved forever motionless.
Pygmalion's rage is still. Victorious
I cannot be, but yours, yours through all storms.

You are a child of Venice, you live here
And stay here; this place is your paradise,
With all Bellini's angels flocking near.

But I – as I glide on, I recognize
I am cheated of a world so great and so dear;
Like the dreams of darkness it dissolves and flies.

ANNETTE
VON DROSTE-HÜLSHOFF

(1797–1848)

THE POND
(DER WEIHER)

So still the pond in morning's gray,
A quiet conscience is not clearer.
When west winds kiss its glassy mirror,
The sedges do not feel it sway.
Above it throbs the dragonfly;
Blue-gold and crimson cross and ply.
And where the sun reflected glances,
The water spider skips and dances.
On the bank a lilied ring scarce blows;
The reedy lullaby will not cease.
A rippling rustle comes and goes,
As though it whispered: peace, peace, peace.

Tr. Herman Salinger   193

THE HOUSE IN THE HEATH
(DAS HAUS IN DER HEIDE)

How peaceful in the afterglow,
Half-hidden in the firred
Heath, is the thatch-roofed hut, bent low
Like huddled bird.

A white-browed heifer in her stall
Nudges its wooden frame,
Snorts, but inhales sweet even-fall,
And is made tame.

Nearby, the garden to protect,
A neat, trimmed hedge of thorn;
One sturdy sunflower stands erect,
Others droop, worn.

There on her knees a quiet child
Bends, seemingly to weed
The lily beds, gently beguiled
By beauty's reed.

At the horizon shepherds lie
Amid the heather; they
Arouse the sleepy, silent sky
With hymned Ave.

And from the barn a cheerful rain
Of hammer blows, the call
Of grinding saw, of rasping plane;
And shavings fall.

The first star rises overhead
Beyond the reaching tree,
And seems to pause, as though to shed
Astronomy.

This is a scene made for the warm
Artistry of the old
Devoted monks: tangible charm
In painted gold.

The carpenter, the shepherd throng,
The maid, the lily fair,
The distant whisper of the song
In peaceful air,

The halo of the stand-still star
Above them all, a hovering light –
May it not be the Savior
Is born this night?

Tr. James Edward Tobin

IN THE GRASS
(IM GRASE)

Sweet repose, sweet reeling in grass,
Enveloped in fragrance of green,
Deep stream, deep deep drunken stream,
When the cloud dissolves in the blue,
When on my tired, swimming head
Sweetly laughter flutters down,
Dear voice murmurs, and trickles
Down like linden blooms onto a grave.

When in the breast then the dead,
Every corpse, stretches and stirs,
Quietly, quietly draws its breath,
Moves its tight-drawn lashes,
Dead love, dead joy, dead time,
All the treasures, immured in the dust
Touch one another, timidly sounding,
As tiny bells wave in the breeze.

Hours, more fleeting are you than the kiss
Of a beam on the sorrowing lake,
Than the song of the passing bird,
That drops like dew from the heights,
Than the glittering beetle's flash,
As it hastes through the sun's path,

Than the ardent clasp of a hand
As it lingers a final time.

Yet, O heaven, this alone
Ever for me: for the song
Of each bird free in the sky
Please, a soul, to fly with him,
But for each scanty beam
This my iridescent hem,
For each warm hand my clasp,
And for every joy my dream.

MOONRISE
(MONDESAUFGANG)

Against the balcony railing I leaned by night
And waited for thee, O thou mildest light.
Above me swam the firmament's high hall,
Melting like cloudy crystal over all;
There stretched the lake before me, shining sheer,
Many a liquid pearl or cloud-born tear.
Dew fell on me, there fell on me the night.
I waited for thee, O thou mildest light.

High up I stood, beside the lindens' comb,
Branches, twigs, and trunks beneath that dome,
In greenery the whir of night moths grew,
Upward glowing a myriad fireflies flew,
And half-asleep, the blossoms fell from heaven.
It seemed to me a heart here found its haven,
A heart, that overfilled with joy and sorrow,
Brought yesteryear's dead image to the morrow.

The darkness climbs, the shadows swell and grow;
Where hidest thou, O where, my dear mild glow?
They came like sinful thoughts that long dissemble,
The wave of firmament appeared to tremble.
The fireflies were an extinguished blur;
Long since the night moths ceased their amorous
        whir.

The mountainous heads alone refused to budge,
A darkling circle, each an ominous judge.

And branches at my feet lisped in the breath
Of wind like warnings dire of eager death;
A humming in the valley, near and far,
Like groan of hosts before the judgment bar
Rose; and I seemed to have accounts to give,
As though a lost life, fearful how to live,
As though, deserted in its guilt and pain,
A heart in misery stood alone in vain.

There, on the waves a silver veil was spread;
Slow, lovely light, thou let thy light be shed,
Rising to stroke each gloomy alpine ledge,
To gentle old men changed each stern-browed judge.
The twitching waves turned to a smiling shimmer,
On every twig a silver drop would glimmer.
To me each drop looked like a little room
Where gleamed, where glowed the friendly lamp of
     home.

O Moon, to me thou art a late-come friend,
Youth adding to one come to this poor end,
Around my memories that faint and fade
Winding a light of life's reflections made.
No sun art thou that blinds and that inspires,
And bleeding ends after a life in fires —

Thou art what to the ailing singer his poem,
Distant, but oh! the mild, mild light of home.

HEINRICH HEINE

(1797–1856)

'IN MAY, THE MAGIC MONTH OF MAY'
('IM WUNDERSCHÖNEN MONAT MAI')

In May, the magic month of May,
When all the buds were springing,
Into my heart the burning
Bright arrow of love came winging.

In May, the magic month of May,
When all the birds were singing,
I told her of my yearning,
My longing and heart-wringing.

'ON WINGS OF SONG'
('FLÜGELN DES GESANGES')

On wings of song, my darling,
I'll carry you off, and we'll go
Where the plains of the Ganges are calling,
To the sweetest place I know.

Red flowers are twining and plaiting
There in the still moonlight:
The lotus flowers are awaiting
Their sister acolyte.

The violets whisper caresses
And gaze to the stars on high;
The rose in secret confesses
Her sweet-scented tales with a sigh.

Around them, listening and blushing,
Dance gentle, subtle gazelles;
And in the distance rushing
The holy river swells.

Oh, let us lie down by it,
Where the moon on the palm tree beams;
And drink deep of love and quiet
And dream our happy dreams.

'THE LOTUS FLOWER'
('DIE LOTOSBLUME ÄNGSTIGT')

The lotus flower is drooping
In the sun's majestic light;
With lowered languid forehead
Dreaming she waits for the night.

The moon he is her lover;
She wakes in his beams' embrace,
To her lover alone unveiling
The innocent flower of her face.

She beams and gleams and glistens
And gazes mutely above;
She weeps scented tears and trembles
With love and the pain of love.

Tr. Hal Draper

'A YOUTH ONCE LOVED'
('EIN JÜNGLING LIEBT EIN MÄDCHEN')

A youth once loved a maiden,
　　Who for another sighed;
This other loves another
　　And takes her for his bride.

And out of spite the maiden
　　Weds the first likely man
That comes her way; and bear it
　　The youth must as he can.

It is an old, old story;
　　Yet is it ever new.
And every time it happens
　　A young heart breaks in two.

'THEY TALKED OF LOVE AND DEVOTION'

('SIE SAßEN UND TRANKEN AM TEETISCH')

They talked of love and devotion
Over the tea and the sweets –
The ladies, of tender emotion;
The men talked like aesthetes.

'True love must be platonic,'
A wizened old councillor cried.
His wife, with a smile ironic,
Bent down her head and sighed.

The canon opened his fat face:
'Love must not be coarse, you know,
It's bad for the health in that case.'
A young girl lisped, 'Why so?'

The countess sadly dissented:
'Oh, love must be wild and free!'
And graciously presented
The baron a cup of tea.

You should have been there, my treasure;
An empty chair stood near.
You'd talk of love and its pleasure
So charmingly, my dear.

LORELEI
('ICH WEIß NICHT, WAS SOLL ES BEDEUTEN')

O what can it be, I wonder,
  This sadness in my breast?
A tale of old torments me;
  It gives my mind no rest.

Cool it has grown, and darker,
  And calmly flows the Rhine;
The tall crag's summit sparkles,
  As evening's rays decline.

And there on high, O wonder!
  A maiden sits most fair.
In golden jewels gleaming,
  She combs her golden hair.

With comb of gold she combs it,
  And sings the while a song.
So fatal its enchantment,
  Its melody so strong.

In anguish wild he hears it,
  The boatman drawing nigh,
The rocks before unseeing,
  He only looks on high.

By floods, methinks, o'ertaken,
   Soon man and boat are gone. –
And that is what the singing
   Of Lorelei hath done!

'THE NIGHT IS STILL, THE STREETS ARE DUMB'
('STILL IST DIE NACHT, ES RUHEN DIE GASSEN')

The night is still, the streets are dumb,
This is the house where dwelt my dear;
Long since she's left the city's hum
But the house stands in the same place here.

Another man stands where the moonbeams lace,
He wrings his hands, eyes turned to the sky.
A shudder runs through me – I see his face:
The man who stands in the moonlight is I.

Pale ghost, twin phantom, hell-begot!
Why do you ape the pain and woe
That racked my heart on this same spot
So many nights, so long ago?

'I CALLED THE DEVIL AND HE CAME'

('ICH RIEF DEN TEUFEL, UND ER KAM')

I called the devil and he came;
I looked him over wonderingly.
He isn't ugly and isn't lame,
He's a likable, charming man, I see,
A man in the prime of life, I surmise,
Obliging and courteous and worldly-wise.
His diplomatic skill is great,
And he talks very nicely on Church and State.
He's somewhat pale — no wonder, I vow,
For he's studying Sanskrit and Hegel now.
His favorite poet is still Fouqué.
He'll put reviewing on the shelf
And do that job no more himself —
Let grandmother Hecate do it today.
For my legal studies he had some praise —
He'd dabbled in law in former days.
He said my friendship made him proud,
Nothing was dearer, and so on — and bowed.
He asked if we hadn't met some place —
At the Spanish embassy over the wine?
And as I looked him full in the face,
I found him an old acquaintance of mine.

'AH, THOSE EYES'
('ACH DIE AUGEN SIND ES WIEDER')

Ah, those eyes – they look as ever
Loving-soft like passionflowers,
And those lips are red as ever,
Lips that sweetened all my hours!

And that voice is low as ever
With the thrill that never faltered!
Only I am not as ever –
Home at last, but changed and altered.

Yet in arms so white and soft where
Love should glow and passion redden,
Now I lie upon her bosom
Unresponding, cold, and leaden.

SEA APPARITION
(SEEGESPENST)

But I leaned over the rail of the vessel,
And dreamy-eyed I lay there gazing
Down into the crystal-clear water,
And gazed down deeper and deeper —
Till deep down on the ocean bottom,
At first like the mist of twilight,
Then gradually resolving in color,
Domes and steeples of churches loomed plainer,
And finally, sun-bright, the whole of a city,
An antique Netherlands city,
Alive with people.
Sedate-mannered men, dressed in black mantles,
With white neck ruffs and with chains of honor,
Bearing long swords and still longer faces,
Go pacing through the bustling plaza
Up the long steps to the ornate town hall
Where marble statues of emperors
Keep vigil with sword and scepter.
Not far away, past long rows of houses
With windows polished like mirrors
And lindens clipped into pyramids,
Rustling in silks young girls are walking,
With slim little figures and flowerlike faces
Modestly circled with neat black bonnets
And outrippling golden hair.

Bright-colored fellows in Spanish dress
Come strutting by, with nods and greetings.
The aged women,
In dark-brown old-fashioned garments,
With hymn books and rosaries in their hands,
Come tripping along in haste
Toward the great cathedral,
Urged on by the churchbells' clanging
And the organ's rumbling voice.

I too am gripped by the distant sound
With a shudder of mystic awe!
An infinite yearning and deep sadness
Steal into my heart,
My heart that's scarcely healed;
I feel as if its wounds are opened
By kisses from belovèd lips
And set again to bleeding –
Hot and red the droplets
Fall long and steadily and slowly
On an ancient house below there
In the deep-sunk sea town,
On an ancient high-gabled house
That stands empty in melancholy,
Save that at the lower window
A maiden sits,
Her head laid on her arm,
Like a poor forsaken child –

And I know you, you poor forsaken child!

So deep, sea-deep indeed
You hid yourself from me
In a childish fancy,
And never more could come up,
And sat a stranger among strange people
For centuries long;
And I the while with sorrow-filled soul
Sought you the whole world over,
And ever I sought you,
My ever-belovèd,
My long-lost belovèd,
At last found, belovèd –
I've found you and now can see once again
Your tender face,
The knowing faithful eyes,
The darling smile –
And never again will I leave you,
And I'm coming right down to you,
And with arms outstretched to embrace you
I plunge down to your heart –

But just in the nick of time
The captain grabbed me by the foot
And pulled me from the rail,
And cried with an angry laugh,
'Doctor, what the devil's got in you?'

MEMORIAL DAY
(GEDÄCHTNISFEIER)

No high mass will they be chanting,
and no *kaddish** will they say.
Nothing will be said nor chanted
on my own memorial day.

But perhaps on such a morning,
if the air is fresh and clean,
there may stroll on the Montmartre
my Mathilde with Pauline.**

With a wreath of everlastings
she will come, my grave adorning,
sighing softly, 'Poor old fellow,'
moist her eye in tearful mourning.

My new home is much too high now;
I can't offer to my dearie
so much as a chair to sit on.
Oh, she sways, her feet are weary.

Walking home, my dear plump darling,
would be much too aggravating.
Look, outside the cemetery,
by the gate, some cabs are waiting.

* Jewish prayer for the dead.
** Companion to Heine's wife, Mathilde.

THE SILESIAN WEAVERS
(DIE SCHLESISCHEN WEBER)

Not a tear in their eye but faces of doom,
And their teeth are bared as they tread the loom:
'Germany, this is your shroud we weave,
The pattern – three curses with no reprieve.
We are weaving, weaving.

'A curse on the idol we prayed to of old
In the torments of hunger, in winter's cold.
We gritted our teeth and hoped in vain,
He fooled us and mocked us and fooled us again.
We are weaving, weaving.

'A curse on the king of the rich and the great
Who was blind to the misery at his gate,
Who squeezed us for every penny we'd got
Till we rose, and like dogs he had us shot.
We are weaving, weaving.

'A curse on the homeland that's no such place
For us whose lives are its shame and disgrace,
Where the bloom is broken and falls by the way,
Where all is corruption, mould and decay.
We are weaving, weaving.

'The creaking loom and the shuttle's flight,
We weave unceasing day and night.
Old Germany, it is your shroud we weave,
The pattern – three curses with no reprieve.
We are weaving, weaving.'

BABYLONIAN SORROWS
(BABYLONISCHE SORGEN)

Death beckons me – O that I could
Leave you, my sweet, in a shadowy wood,
In some distant forest of darksome firs,
Where wild wolves howl, where the hawk scarce stirs
The air, and the wild sow roams the floor,
The lawful wife of the blond wild boar.

Death beckons me. How much better 'twould be
To leave you alone on the lone high sea,
Where the wind is mad and comes whipping wild
The waves into frenzy, O my wife, my child,
And where the monsters out of the deep
Rise from their accustomed sleep,
Where sharks and crocodiles, green and dim
And open-mawed wallow and float and swim.
Believe me, Mathilde, my wife and child,
Not half so dangerous is the wild
And angry sea, the forest wind-bent
As this place where we have pitched our tent!
However vile the wolf and the hawk,
The sharks and monsters of which I talk,
More vile are the beasts, more filled with guile
Which Paris harbors all the while.
Yes, dancing, glancing pearl beyond price,
Paris, the devils' paradise,

The angels' hell – that I leave you here
Enrages and maddens and blinds me, dear!

Around my bed the buzzing flies
Make sport of me; above my eyes
They settle and on my nose – foul flock!
Some even have human faces; they mock
At me. One delights to sit and nod
With an elephant's trunk like a Hindu god.
All day in my brain it has rumbled and cracked;
I believe some luggage is being packed,
And my reason is leaving – alas, what woe!
Before I myself am ready to go.

NIKOLAUS LENAU

(1802–50)

THE OAK GROVE
(DER EICHWALD)

I trod that day the sacred shadows
Of an oak grove; along the way
I heard a brook by wild flowers flowing
With still voice hushed, as children pray.

A blissful awe had seized my spirit.
The forest accents, rustling, low,
Seemed as by stealth to hint a secret
It was not yet my right to know,

Seemed on the brink of revelation
Of what God's love has thought and willed —
Then suddenly the forest trembled
As at God's nearness — and was stilled.

Tr. Dwight Durling

'THE EVENING WIND IN THE TREETOPS'
('DER NACHTWIND HAT IN DEN BÄUMEN')

The evening wind in the treetops
Has ceased its rustling now,
The birds are sitting and dreaming
Together on the bough.

The distant, trickling streamlet,
Since other sounds are done,
Audibly, wave upon wavelet,
Now lets its waters run.

And when what is near falls silent,
Then come in doleful train
Soft-footed recollections
And, weeping, part again.

That everything dies and passes
Is a truth we all well know,
But of our bitter sadness
None yet has stanched the flow.

PLEA
(BITTE)

Rest upon me, eye of darkness,
Practice now your every might,
Never fathomed in your beauty,
Solemn, gentle, dreaming night.

By the magic of your darkness
Take from me this world away,
That above my life forever
Lonely you may keep your sway.

Tr. George C. Schoolfield

EDUARD MÖRIKE

(1804–75)

IN SPRING
(IM FRÜHLING)

I lie here on the hill of spring;
The cloud becomes my wing;
A bird flies away at my feet.
Ah tell me, all-singular love,
Where you take rest that with you I may stay;
But you and the breezes, you have no retreat.

My spirit like the sunflower stands wide open,
Yearning,
Out-turning
In loving and hoping.
Spring, what goads you, possessed?
When shall I be at rest?

I watch the motion of the cloud and stream;
The golden kiss of the sunbeam
Into my heart's blood pierces deep;
My eyes, by potent lethargies
Sung shut, might seem asleep,
But the ear catches still the sound of bees.

I think of this and think of that,
I long, and do not rightly know for what,
Half it delights me, half dismays;
Say, heart, O phrase,
What recollection do you weave
Out of dawn mist the gold-green branches leave?
Old, unnamable days!

TO AN AEOLIAN HARP
(AN EINE ÄOLSHARFE)

Tu semper urges flebilibus modis
Mysten ademptum: nec tibi Vespero
  Surgente decedunt amores,
    Nec rapidum fugiente Solem.
        Horace

Leaning against the ivy wall
Of this old terrace,
You, instrument mysterious
Of a muse born of the air,
Begin,
And again begin
Your melodious lament.

Winds, you are coming from far,
Ah, from the fresh green
Hill he is under,
The boy I loved so well.
And combing springtime blossoms as you pass,
Drenched with perfumes,
How sweetly you press at my heart,
And whisper among the strings,
Ondrawn by sonorous sorrow's moan,
Rising in the motion of my grief,
And dying away again.

But all at once,
As the wind heaves a heavier sigh,
A tender cry from the harp
Repeats, sweetly startling me,
The sudden tremor through my soul;
And here – the full rose loosens, shaken,
At my feet all its petals.

THE BEAUTIFUL BEECH TREE
(DIE SCHÖNE BUCHE)

Hidden deep in the wood I know of a place where a
    beech tree
  Stands, in beauty beyond any a picture can show.
Clean and smooth it rises up, strong-bodied, aloof,
  Swathed in silken allure none of its neighbors can
    touch.
Round it, far as the noble tree puts branches forth,
  Grows, delighting the eye, turf in a ring of green;
With radius always constant it circles the trunk in the
    center,
  Artlessly nature herself shaped this charming
    surround.
First it is fringed by wispy bushes, further back
  Trees with towering boles fend the heavenly blue.
Fulsome the dark oak grows and beside it the virginal
  Crest of the birch that, shy, sways in the golden
    light.
Only the spot where the path disappears, half-hidden
    by rocks,
  Out of the glade gives a hint of open country
    beyond.
— Not long since, walking alone, as the summery
    shapes,
  New, had lured me away from the path and I lost
    myself

In the bushes, a friendly spirit, the listening god of
    the grove,
  Led me here for the first time and in wonder I
    stood.
What delight! It was the moment of high noon,
  Everything was hushed, even the birds in the
    leaves.
And I was hesitant still to tread on the exquisite
    carpet;
  A ceremony it seemed, at length as I stole across.
Then, as I leaned against the trunk (its canopy billows
  Out not much overhead), freely my widening gaze
Followed the burning ray of the sun as it ran in a
    circle,
  Edging the shadowy round, almost measuring it.
There I stood, without moving, listening deep in
    myself
  To the demonic stillness, calm unfathomable.
With you enclosed in this magic circle of sun my only
  Thought, O solitude, my only feeling was you.

ON A LAMP
(AUF EINE LAMPE)

Not yet disturbed, O lovely lamp, you still adorn,
Gracefully suspended here on slender chains,
The ceiling of this pleasance, near-forgotten now.
On your white marble bowl, around whose rim is
    twined
A wreath of ivy leaves in greenish golden bronze,
Children happily join to dance a roundelay.
What charm throughout! laughing, yet the whole
    form
Ringed by a gentle flowing spirit of seriousness.
A work of art, the genuine thing. Who notices it?
Yet blithely beauty seems to shine in self-content.

Tr. Christopher Middleton

REFLECT, MY SOUL
(DENK' ES, O SEELE)

A sapling fir grows – where?
Who knows, in forest,
A rosebush, who says,
And in which garden?
They are sought out,
Reflect, my soul,
Upon your grave to take root
And to stablish.

Two young black colts are grazing
On the common,
On their way back home
They jump and canter.
They'll go at solemn pace
To draw your body;
Perhaps, perhaps ere
On their hooves
The shoes wear off
That I see gleaming.

AT MIDNIGHT
(UM MITTERNACHT)

Serene, her landing; dreaming still,
Night leans against the wall of hills;
She watches now time's golden balance cease
From tilting, views the poise of scales at peace.
   And gushing fresher, the springs flow along,
    They sing for the Mother, for Night, their song
      Of the day,
      Of the day that has been today.

So old, this slumber-song of yore,
She's tired of it, she heeds no more;
To her, a sweeter ring's the blue of sky,
Their yoke swung level as the Hours fleet by,
   But always the word is borne on by the springs,
    And while it is sleeping the water still sings
      Of the day,
      Of the day that has been today.

Tr. Joseph B. Dallett

TO A CHRISTMAS-ROSE (*Helleborus niger*)
(AUF EINE CHRISTBLUME)

I

Child of the wood, half-sister to the lily,
You whom I've sought so vainly in the past,
In this remote, deserted, wintry graveyard,
O lovely thing, I find you now at last!

By whose hand tended, glowing here so fair,
I know not, nor whose grave it is you guard;
If of a youth, by fortune was he blest,
And if a maiden's, bliss was her reward.

Deep in the night-clad grove, illumed by snow,
Near where the harmless, grazing roe-bucks roam,
Against the chapel, by the crystal pool,
I sought the mystic kingdom of your home.

You are the moon's fair daughter, not the sun's. –
To you the bliss of other blooms were death.
The sweet, balm-laden coolness of the sky
Feeds your chaste body, ripe and mild of breath.

There lurks, embedded in your golden heart,
A scent, that scarcely makes its presence known;
Such fragrance spread, by angels' hands caressed,
The blessèd Virgin-Mother's wedding gown.

Five single crimson drops would suit you well,
To call to mind the Passion's sacred scene;
But child-like, you adorn at Christmas-tide
Your garment white with tinges of pale green.

The fairy elf, that through the shining dell
At midnight dances lightly on its way,
Distrusting your effulgent mystery,
Peers, silent, from afar, and darts away.

II

A flower-bud sleeps in winter's soil embraced,
The butterfly, that soon on nights of spring
O'er bush and hill will wave its velvet wing;
Your syrup's nectar it will never taste,

But yet who knows? Perhaps its spirit rare,
Long after summer's lustre has been spent,
Drunk with the silent sweetness of your scent,
Not seen by me, may haunt you blooming here.

Tr. Geoffrey Herbert Chase

PRAYER
(GEBET)

Send me what you will, Lord,
Be it pain or pleasure;
Each in welcome measure
From your hands is poured.

Do not overwhelm me, pray,
With sorrow or delight;
The fairest share, it seems,
Of either ever lay
Between extremes.

RICHARD WAGNER

(1813–88)

SO LET US DIE
(SO STÜRBEN WIR)
from *Tristan and Isolde*

So let us die
And never part,
Die united,
Heart to heart,
Never waking,
Never fearing,
Nameless,
Endless rapture sharing,
Each to each devoted,
In love alone abiding!

O eternal night,
Blessed night.
Holy noble
Night of love!
When you enfold us,
When we are blessed,
How could we be wakened
From you without dismay?
Now banish all fearing
Sweetest death,
Longed for and hoped for

Love in death!
Thine arms around me,
Thine alone,
Love sacred and glowing,
From all waking grief released.
How to grasp it,
How to leave it,
Sweet enchantment,
Far from sunlight,
Far from day
And parting sorrow.
No illusion,
Tender yearning!
No more fearing,
Sweetly burning,
No more grieving,
Ah, expiring;
No more pining,
Night-enfolded!
Undivided,
Never parting,
Thine alone,
Ever thine
In boundless realms of rapture,
Blessed endless dreaming:
Thou (I) Isolde,
Tristan, I (thou),
No more Tristan.

No more Isolde!
Ever nameless,
Never parting,
Newly learning,
Newly burning;
Endless ever
Joined in joy,
Ever-glowing love,
Highest holy love.

ACKNOWLEDGMENTS AND SOURCES

Thanks are due to the following copyright holders for permission to reprint:

CLEMENS BRENTANO: 'Slumber Song' / 'Wiegenlied' (tr. Anne Jennings) and 'The Spinstress' Song' / 'Der Spinnerin Lied' (tr. Alexander Gode) from *Anthology of German Poetry Through the 19th Century*, ed. Alexander Gode and Frederick Ungar (New York: Ungar, 1964, 1972). Bloomsbury Publishing. 'Holy Night, Holy Night!' / 'Heil'ge Nacht, heil'ge Nacht!' (tr. David B. Dickens) and 'Echoes of Beethoven's Music' / 'Nachklänge Beethovenscher Musik' (tr. George C. Schoolfield) from *German Poetry from 1750 to 1900*, ed. Robert M. Browning, foreword by Michael Hamburger (New York: Continuum, 1984). Bloomsbury Publishing. 'Evening Serenade' and 'The Forest' from *German Verse from the 12th to the 20th Century in English Translation* by J. W. Thomas. The University of North Carolina Studies in Germanic Languages and Literatures, No. 44. Copyright © 1964 by the University of North Carolina Press. Used by permission of the publisher. 'Lore Lay' and 'Lord! Within Thy Peace I Rest Me' (tr. Mabel Cotterell) from *An Anthology of German Poetry from Hölderlin to Rilke in English Translation with German Originals*, ed Angel Flores (New York: Anchor, 1960).

ADALBERT VON CHAMISSO: 'Lord Byron's Last Love' / 'Lord Byrons letzte Liebe' (tr. Michael Ferber) from Michael Ferber, *European Romantic Poetry* (New York, London: Pearson Longman, 2005). 'The Soldier' / 'Der Soldat' (tr. Geoffrey Herbert Chase) from *Poems from the German*, *volume two: Further Selected Lyrics and Ballads from Goethe to Hofmannsthal* (Edinburgh and London: William Blackwood & Sons Ltd, 1961).

ANNETTE VON DROSTE-HÜLSHOFF: 'In the Grass'/ 'Im Grase' (tr. Jane K. Brown) from Michael Ferber, *European Romantic Poetry* (New York, London: Pearson Longman, 2005). 'The Pond' / 'Der Weiher' and 'Moonrise' / 'Mondesaufgang' (tr. Herman Salinger); and 'The House in the Heath' / 'Das Haus in der Heide' (tr. James Edward Tobin) from *An Anthology of German Poetry from Hölderlin to Rilke in English Translation with German Originals*, ed. Angel Flores (New York: Anchor, 1960).

JOSEPH FREIHERR VON EICHENDORFF: 'Dialogue in the Forest' / 'Waldgespräch' (tr. Gerd Gillhoff), 'The Joyful Traveller' / 'Der frohe Wandersmann' (tr. Stewart H. Benedict), 'Night' / 'Die Nachtblume' (tr. Isabel S. MacInnes), 'The Hermit' / 'Der Einsiedler' (tr. Meno Spann) and 'Wishing Wand' / 'Wünschelrute' (tr. Alison Turner) from *Anthology of German Poetry Through the 19th Century*, ed. Alexander Gode and Frederick Ungar (New York: Ungar, 1964, 1972) Bloomsbury Publishing. 'Death Wish' / 'Todeslust' and 'Memento mori' / 'Memento mori!' (tr. Robert M. Browning) from *German Poetry from 1750 to 1900*, ed. Robert M. Browning, foreword by Michael Hamburger (New York: Continuum, 1984). Bloomsbury Publishing. 'On the Death of my Child' / 'Auf meines Kindes Tod', translated by Kate Flores. The Estate of Angel Flores. From *An Anthology of German Poetry from Hölderlin to Rilke in English Translation with German Originals*, ed. Angel Flores (New York: Anchor, 1960). 'The Broken Ring' from *German Verse from the 12th*

FRIEDRICH VON HARDENBERG: *Hymns to Night / Hymnen an die Nacht* II and VI ['Longing for Death' / 'Sehnsucht nach dem Tode'] (tr. Robert M. Browning) from *German Poetry from 1750 to 1900*, ed. Robert M. Browning, foreword by Michael Hamburger (New York: Continuum, 1984). Bloomsbury Publishing. 'Maria' and 'The Hermit's Song' from *German Verse from the 12th to the 20th Century in English Translation* by J. W. Thomas. The University of North Carolina Studies in Germanic Languages and Literatures, No. 44. Copyright © 1964 by the University of North Carolina Press. Used by permission of the publisher. *Sacred Songs* X, 'There Come Such Troubled Hours' / 'Es gibt so bange Zeiten' from *An Anthology of German Poetry from Hölderlin to Rilke in English Translation with German Originals*, ed. Angel Flores (New York: Anchor, 1960).

HEINRICH HEINE: 'Memorial Day' / 'Gedächtnisfeier' (tr. Max Knight) from *German Poetry from 1750 to 1900*, ed. Robert M. Browning, foreword by Michael Hamburger (New York: Continuum, 1984). Bloomsbury Publishing. 'Babylonian Sorrows' / 'Babylonische Sorgen' (tr. Herman Salinger) from *An Anthology of German Poetry from Hölderlin to Rilke in English Translation with German Originals*, ed. Angel Flores (New York: Anchor, 1960). 'In May, the magic month of May' / 'Im wunderschönen Monat Mai', 'On wings of song' / 'Flügeln des Gesanges', 'The lotus flower'/ 'Die Lotosblume ängstigt', 'They talked of love and devotion' / 'Sie sassen und tranken am Teetisch', 'The night is still, the streets are dumb' / 'Still ist die Nacht, es ruhen die Gassen',

JUSTINUS KERNER: 'Oppressive Dream' / 'Der schwere Traum [Ikaros]' (tr. John Fitzell) from *German Poetry from 1750–1900*, ed. Robert M. Browning, foreword by Michael Hamburger (New York: Continuum, 1984). Bloomsbury Publishing. 'The Saw-Mill' / 'Der Wanderer in der Sägemühle' (tr. Geoffrey Herbert Chase) from *Poems from the German, volume two: Further Selected Lyrics and Ballads from Goethe to Hofmannsthal* (Edinburgh and London: William Blackwood & Sons Ltd, 1961).

NIKOLAUS LENAU: 'Plea' / 'Bitte' (tr. George C. Schoolfield) from *Anthology of German Poetry Through the 19th Century*, ed. Alexander Gode and Frederick Ungar (New York: Ungar, 1964, 1972). Bloomsbury Publishing. ['The evening wind in the treetops'] / ['Nachtwind hat in den Bäumen'] (tr. Robert M. Browning) from *German Poetry from 1750 to 1900*, ed. Robert M. Browning, foreword by Michael Hamburger (New York: Continuum, 1984). Bloomsbury Publishing. 'The Oak Grove' / 'Der Eichwald' (tr. Dwight Durling) from *An Anthology of German Poetry from Hölderlin to Rilke in English Translation with German Originals*, ed. Angel Flores (New York: Anchor, 1960).

SOPHIE MEREAU: 'Spring / Frühling' and 'To a Trellised Tree' / 'An einen Baum am Spalier' from Jeannine Blackwell and Susanne Zantop, *Bitter Healing: German Women Writers from 1700 to 1830: An Anthology* (Lincoln and London: University of Nebraska Press, 1990). Verse translations by Walter Arndt.

EDUARD MÖRIKE: 'At Midnight' / 'Um Mitternacht' (tr. Joseph B. Dallett) from *German Poetry from 1750 to 1900*, ed. Robert M. Browning, foreword by Michael Hamburger (New

York: Continuum, 1984). Bloomsbury Publishing. 'Reflect, My Soul'/ 'Denk' es, o Seele' (tr. Roger Paulin). Reprinted with permission from the translator. 'To an Aeolian Harp' / 'An eine Äolsharfe', 'The Beautiful Beech Tree' / 'Die schöne Buche', 'On a Lamp' / 'Auf eine Lampe' and 'Prayer' / 'Gebet' from *Friedrich Hölderlin, Eduard Mörike: Selected Poems*, translated and with an introduction by Christopher Middleton (University of Chicago Press, 1972). 'In Spring' / 'Im Frühling' (tr. Vernon Watkins) from *An Anthology of German Poetry from Hölderlin to Rilke in English Translation with German Originals*, ed. Angel Flores (New York: Anchor, 1960). "To a Christmas-Rose' / 'Auf eine Christblume' (tr. Geoffrey Herbert Chase) from *Poems from the German, volume two: Further Selected Lyrics and Ballads from Goethe to Hofmannsthal* (Edinburgh and London: William Blackwood & Sons Ltd, 1961).

WILHELM MÜLLER: 'The Journeyman's Song' / 'Wanderschaft' (tr. Francis Owen) from *Anthology of German Poetry Through the 19th Century*, ed. Alexander Gode and Frederick Ungar (New York: Ungar, 1964, 1972). Bloomsbury Publishing. 'The Linden Tree'/ 'Der Lindenbaum' (tr. John Fitzell) from *German Poetry from 1750 to 1900*, ed. Robert M. Browning, foreword by Michael Hamburger (New York: Continuum, 1984). Bloomsbury Publishing.

AUGUST GRAF VON PLATEN-HALLERMÜNDE: 'Fain Would I Live in Safest Freedom' / 'Ich möchte gern mich frei bewahren', 'Truest of Sages are You to Me' / 'Du bist der wahre Weise mir' and 'Venetian Sonnets' / 'Sonette aus Venedig' II and VIII from *Collected Translations* by Edwin Morgan, Carcanet Press, 1996. Reprinted with permission.

FRIEDRICH RÜCKERT: 'Now the sun prepares to rise as brightly' / 'Nun will die Sonn' so hell aufgeh'n' from *The Penguin Book of Lieder*, ed. and trans. Siegbert Prawer (Harmondsworth: Penguin, 1964). 'Closing Song' / 'Schlusslied', translated by Charlotte Lee. Translation copyright © by Charlotte Lee. Reprinted with permission from the translator. 'My Soul, My Heart' and 'O Stop with Me' from *German Verse from the 12th to the 20th Century in English Translation* by J. W. Thomas. The University of North Carolina Studies in Germanic Languages and Literatures, No. 44. Copyright © 1964 by the University of North Carolina Press. Used by permission of the publisher.

FRIEDRICH SCHILLER: 'The Ideal and Life' / 'Das Ideal und das Leben' translated by Richard Winston. Copyright © Krishna Winston. Reprinted with permission. 'Nenia' / 'Nänie' (tr. Alexander Gode) from *Anthology of German Poetry Through the 19th Century*, ed. Alexander Gode and Frederick Ungar (New York: Ungar, 1964, 1972). Bloomsbury Publishing. 'Evening' and 'Mountain Song' from *German Verse from the 12th to the 20th Century in English Translation* by J. W. Thomas. The University of North Carolina Studies in Germanic Languages and Literatures, No. 44. Copyright © 1964 by the University of North Carolina Press. Used by permission of the publisher.

AUGUST WILHELM SCHLEGEL: 'The Sonnet' / 'Das Sonett' (tr. Roger Paulin). Reprinted with permission from the translator. 'Evening Song for the Distant Beloved' / 'Abendlied für die Entfernte' (tr. Richard Wigmore) from

Richard Wigmore, *Schubert: The Complete Song Texts* (London: Gollancz, 1992). Reproduced with permission of the Licensor through PLSclear.

FRIEDRICH SCHLEGEL: 'Sunset' and 'The Boatman' from Richard Wigmore, *Schubert: The Complete Song Texts* (London: Gollancz, 1992). Reproduced with permission of the Licensor through PLSclear.

LUDWIG TIECK: 'Love' / 'Liebe' (tr. Herman Salinger) from *German Poetry from 1750 to 1900*, ed. Robert M. Browning, foreword by Michael Hamburger (New York: Continuum, 1984). Bloomsbury Publishing. 'Wonder of Love' / 'Wunder der Liebe' (tr. Roger Paulin). Reprinted with permission from the translator. "Sweet Darling, Rest in the Shade' / 'Schaflied' from *The Penguin Book of Lieder*, ed. and trans. Siegbert Prawer (Harmondsworth: Penguin, 1964).

LUDWIG UHLAND: 'On the Death of a Child' / 'Auf den Tod eines Kindes' (tr. Oliver Brown) from *Anthology of German Poetry Through the 19th Century*, ed. Alexander Gode and Frederick Ungar (New York: Ungar, 1964, 1972). Bloomsbury Publishing. 'The Smith' and 'Spring Faith' from *German Verse from the 12th to the 20th Century in English Translation* by J. W. Thomas. The University of North Carolina Studies in Germanic Languages and Literatures, No. 44. Copyright © 1964 by the University of North Carolina Press. Used by permission of the publisher. 'The Chapel' / 'Die Kapelle', 'The Dream' / 'Der Traum' and 'The Gossamer' / 'Der Sommerfaden' are taken from Charles R. Lambert, *Poems and Translations from the German of Goethe, Schiller, Chamisso, Uhland, Rückert, Platen, etc.* (London, 1850).